THE EVENING STANDARD COOKBOOK

Delia Smith is one of the most popular
cookery experts writing today.

Justly famous for her phenomenally
successful BBC TV series, *Delia
Smith's Cookery Course*, and for her
regular column in the *Evening News*
(and before that in the *Evening
Standard*), she has a huge and
devoted following.

THE EVENING STANDARD COOKBOOK
is a classic of the cookery world. Its
purpose is not to present great
gastronomic discoveries but
sensible ways of making everyday
meals more attractive and interesting.

D0715311

The Evening Standard Cookbook

Delia Smith

CORONET BOOKS
Hodder and Stoughton

Copyright © 1974 Beaverbrook Newspapers Limited

First published in Great Britain
1974 by Beaverbrook Newspapers
Limited

Coronet Edition 1978
Seventh impression 1983

Printed and bound in Great Britain for
Hodder and Stoughton Paperbacks, a
division of Hodder and Stoughton Ltd.,
Mill Road, Dunton Green, Sevenoaks,
Kent (Editorial Office: 47 Bedford
Square, London, WC1 3DP) by
Richard Clay (The Chaucer Press) Ltd., Bungay, Suffolk

ISBN 0 340 23094 0

Contents

Preface

Here, by request, is a collection of recipes which have appeared in the *Evening Standard* over the past two years. I say by request, because so many kind readers have written asking for it – some of them with hard-luck stories to touch the coldest heart. I recall one lady whose clipping of Poor Man's Stroganoff had become so yoghurt-splattered she couldn't read it any more. And the gentleman who had finally tracked down some juniper berries for his oxtail casserole, but alas he had lost the recipe!

To them, to all those whose tales of woe about tatty, yellowing cut-outs or papers that were thrown out 'in error' have moved me deeply, and to all faithful recipe-followers, this book is dedicated.

When I began these recipes for the *Evening Standard* I knew that with a recipe every day, plus a lengthier Saturday column, I would have the opportunity to fit in something for everyone, and that is what I have tried very hard to do – with recipes for beginners, recipes for more experienced cooks, and even a few cheating recipes for reluctant cooks.

Always on weekdays I tend to have city commuters at the back of my mind – perhaps because for years I was myself a commuter. Therefore I try to keep the recipes uncomplicated – the daily offerings are not intended to be great discoveries in the field of gastronomy, but rather ways of making everyday family meals more attractive and interesting. Being an uncomplicated cook myself, I firmly believe it's not always necessary to spend hours of hard labour to produce something that tastes good. I also believe that cooking is so riddled with rumours and old wives' tales, it's sometimes worth questioning some of the 'rules' to find out whether they are valid or not.

People are always asking how I think of seven recipes a week. The answer is simple. The day I run out of ideas is the day when I know everything there is to know about cooking. And knowing everything there is to know about such a vast subject as cooking looks to me to be a very long way off. Meanwhile, I'll keep on searching for new ideas, and I hope *you'll* keep on cooking.

I should like to thank Caroline Liddall for her invaluable assistance in testing many of the daily recipes published in the *Evening Standard* over the past two years, and Helen Howard for her help in assembling the recipes for inclusion in this book.

1974   Delia Smith

1 Soups, Hot and Cold

Soup before a dinner, it has been said, is like a portico to a palace or an overture to an opera. On the other hand the Marquis de Cussy (so Kettner says in his *Book of the Table*) called it a preface, and maintained that a good book could do without a preface. When the great chef Carème (on his death-bed) heard what the Marquis had said, he groaned over this heresy and among his last words were: 'Why should he wage war on soup? I cannot

understand a dinner without it. I hold soup to be the well-beloved of the stomach.'

Nowadays, of course, people don't get very emotional about soup and I think Carême on his death-bed would have groaned louder and longer had he caught a glimpse of our generation, with our tin-openers and our chemically flavoured instant packets. The well-beloved of the stomach has now become largely a convenient way to stave off the pangs of hunger around lunch-time.

Yet, some home-made soups are incredibly easy to make, and many vegetable soups take little longer than 30 or 40 minutes, if you have a liquidizer and can cut out the sieving time. Almost any home-made soup, in my opinion, is infinitely preferable to anything that comes out of a tin or packet. More than that, when made with home-made stock it is a positive luxury – if only because that is so rare. If you have a little time and an obliging butcher to give you some beef bones, then do make some stock for your soups, and enjoy one of the really good things of life at very little cost.

Basic Stock

4 lb beef shin bones (in pieces)
1 lb veal knuckle bones (in pieces)
1 Spanish onion, peeled and quartered
2 large carrots, peeled and cut into large chunks

2 celery stalks with leaves, cut into halves
1 small bunch parsley stalks
1 bay leaf
10 whole black peppercorns
1 blade of mace
1 heaped teaspoon salt
1 level teaspoon sugar

For this recipe you will need a large cooking pot, about 6 quarts capacity.

First, pre-heat the oven to gas mark 8 (450°F), then place the bones in a meat roasting tin with the quartered onion and chunks of carrot. Don't put in any fat, just place the tin on the highest shelf in the oven and leave it there for around 45 minutes, to let the bones and vegetables get nicely browned (turning them now and then to brown evenly).

Have some boiling water ready, then when the bones are browned, transfer them together with the browned onion and carrots to your cooking pot, pour on about a pint of boiling water, then add a further 7 pints cold water – throwing in the celery, bay leaf, mace, peppercorns and parsley stalks at the same time.

Now bring the liquid very slowly up to simmering point, add the salt and the sugar, skim off any scum that has risen to the surface, then put a lid almost on and let the stock simmer as gently as possible for 4 to 5 hours. Putting the lid half, or almost, on the pan ensures that during the simmering the liquid will reduce, giving the stock a better and more concentrated flavour.

When the stock is ready, strain it into a clean pan and leave it to cool – once the stock is quite cold you can remove the layer of fat which will have formed on the surface (keep it for dripping), and the stock is then ready for use. You can either discard the bones or top them up with more water, just as you wish.

This is a basic brown beef stock, but you can of course make a light stock, by using all veal bones instead of beef and by dispensing with the browning operation in the oven. The vegetables, seasonings and proportions would be exactly the same as above. A light stock would be more suitable for pale soups and sauces.

Chicken stock

Chicken stock is very good for soups and sauces too. Place the carcass in a saucepan together with the giblets (or giblet stock) and skin, etc. Add a carrot, an onion and some celery, a bay loaf, peppercorns, parsley stalks and salt, then cover with water and simmer very gently for about 2 to 2½ hours.

Asparagus Cream Soup

For four to six people:

2 lb asparagus	1¾ pints chicken stock
2 oz butter	¼ pint double cream
1 slightly rounded tablespoon flour	Salt and freshly milled black pepper
1 medium onion, finely chopped	

Prepare the asparagus by cutting away and discarding the tough, stringy white ends of the stalks, then chop the green parts (including the heads) into 1-inch lengths, and wash them in cold water.

Next melt the butter in a large saucepan over a gentle heat and cook the chopped onion in it for 5 minutes, keeping the heat low to prevent the onion colouring at all. Stir the asparagus into the melted butter and onion, then put a lid on and let it sweat for about 10 minutes, giving it a stir now and then.

Sprinkle in a tablespoon of flour, stir again to soak up the juices and add the hot chicken stock a little at a time, stirring after each addition.

When all the stock is in, bring to simmering point, season with salt and freshly milled black pepper and, keeping the heat low, let the soup barely simmer for about 20 to 25 minutes, until the asparagus is soft.

You can now either make a purée in a liquidizer, or press the soup through a sieve.

Taste to check the seasoning, stir in the cream and re-heat gently (or cool and serve well chilled).

Avocado and Prawn Soup

For four people:

2 medium-sized avocados	½ onion, sliced
½ lb prawns (in their shells)	8 peppercorns
¼ lb white fish (cod or haddock)	1 bay leaf
¼ pint soured cream	Salt and nutmeg
½ lemon	

Start by preparing the prawns, first taking off the shells – any roe clinging to them can be rinsed off under a running tap. Keep the prawns in a cool place, then place all the shells and debris in a saucepan with the white fish, onion, peppercorns, bay leaf, a small strip of lemon peel and a little salt.

Measure a pint of water into the saucepan, then put a lid on, bring to simmering point, and simmer for 45 minutes. Then strain off the stock and allow it to cool.

To prepare the avocados, cut them in halves, remove the stones, then cut them into quarters. Now take a dessertspoon and, holding each avocado quarter fast at one end, scrape off all the flesh, especially the very green part right next to the skin.

Place all the avocado flesh in a large bowl, add the juice of half a lemon, some salt and freshly milled black pepper. Now mash to a pulp with a fork. It does not have to be a smooth pulp yet.

Now add the soured cream and mash again to blend it in. At this point, if you have a liquidizer you can make a smooth purée, and if not, you can press the whole lot through a fine sieve.

Either way, as soon as you have your smooth avocado purée you can then gradually stir into it the fish stock, but not all of it, probably about ¾ pint. Now taste to see if any more salt or pepper is needed, and add a little scraping of nutmeg.

Then add the shelled prawns, chopped up a bit if they are very large. Serve the soup either well-chilled or gently heated. Thinly sliced brown bread and butter makes a good accompaniment.

Italian Bean and Pasta Soup

To serve six people:

½ lb Italian white haricot beans
¼ lb small-cut macaroni
2 tablespoons tomato purée
1 large onion, chopped small
2 cloves garlic, chopped small

2 oz freshly grated Parmesan
  cheese
2 tablespoons olive oil
Salt and freshly milled black
  pepper

If you have the time, soak the beans overnight in 3 pints cold water. If not, bring them to the boil and let them soak for about two hours. Then gently fry the onion in olive oil for 10 minutes or so. Add the chopped garlic and tomato purée, stir for a minute or two, then pour in the beans and the water they were soaking in. Now bring the soup to the boil, cover and simmer very gently for 3 hours. When the time is up, season with salt and pepper and put half the soup through a sieve or blend in a liquidizer. Return the puréed half to the pan, bring to simmering point, add the macaroni and simmer for a further 12 minutes. Serve the soup with lots of freshly grated Parmesan cheese to sprinkle over.

Carrot and Tarragon Soup

To serve four to six people:

1½ lb carrots (these should be
  brightly coloured and not too
  old)
1 medium potato
1 medium onion
(all the above should be peeled
  and chopped small)

2 pints chicken stock (made
  with a cube)
2 oz butter
A couple of pinches dried
  tarragon
Salt
Freshly milled black pepper

Melt the butter, stir in the vegetables, put the lid on and allow to sweat over a low heat for 10 minutes; then add the stock plus seasonings and simmer for approximately 25 minutes. Finally, liquidize the soup or press through a sieve.

When re-heating the soup taste to check the seasoning and add a couple of pinches of crumpled dried tarragon leaves – don't be tempted to add more because it's very strong and too much will mask the fresh flavour of the carrots.

An alternative, and more substantial, version of this soup would be to add some bacon rinds during the cooking, extract them before liquidizing and garnish the soup with chopped fried bacon and cubes of crisp fried bread (and no tarragon).

Celery Soup with Nutmeg

This recipe includes nutmeg, which gives it an extra specially good flavour. Quantities for four servings:

1 head celery (about 2 lb)	½ pint milk
1 pint stock (chicken cube stock will do)	1 tablespoon single cream
1 large onion, chopped small	2 oz butter
1 medium potato, chopped small	Pepper, salt and whole nutmeg

Wash the celery very thoroughly, discarding any obviously stringy bits, and chop it very small. The leaf-tops are important to the flavour so chop these up too.

Take a good thick saucepan and slowly melt the butter, then add the onion and potato. Cook them for a minute or two, then add them to the celery. Stir well, add salt and freshly milled pepper, put the lid on the saucepan and leave it to sweat over a low heat for 10 minutes.

Now pour in the stock and milk and let it all simmer gently for about 30 to 40 minutes. When it is cooked, strain the liquid into a soup tureen, rub half the vegetables through a sieve into the stock, then put the other half in as they are. Pour the soup back into the saucepan, add a few good gratings of whole nutmeg, reheat and add the cream just before serving.

Chicken Soup with Vegetables

The ingredients for about six helpings are:

1 chicken carcass (skin, debris, everything that is left)	1 bay leaf
	A bunch parsley stalks
1 onion, quartered	A few celery tops
1 carrot	Salt and pepper

Place all the above in a large cooking pot, break the carcass in half, pour in enough water to cover, and bring to the boil. Skim, then simmer very gently for about $2\frac{1}{2}$ hours.

Meanwhile prepare, clean and chop small:

2 large (or 4 small) leeks	2 medium carrots
2 sticks celery	2 medium potatoes
1 small turnip	

When the stock is nearly ready, melt some chicken fat or butter in another large saucepan, then add all the prepared vegetables.

Stir them round, then put a lid on and let them sweat over a very gentle heat for 10 to 15 minutes – then add the strained stock and simmer for a further 15 to 20 minutes, or until the vegetables are soft.

Now you can either liquidize the soup or sieve it. Re-heat and taste to check the seasoning before serving. (If you happen to have any giblet gravy left over, add it to the soup right at the end.)

Chilled Cucumber Soup

For four to six people:

2 medium-sized firm young English cucumbers	1 dessertspoon lemon juice
$\frac{1}{2}$ pint natural yoghurt	1 teaspoon fresh chopped mint
$\frac{1}{4}$ pint soured cream	A little cold milk
1 large clove garlic, crushed	Salt
	Freshly milled black pepper

First, peel the cucumbers and slice them thinly. Reserve a few paper-thin slices for a garnish and place the rest in the liquidizer. Add the yoghurt, soured cream and garlic, then blend at the highest speed till smooth. Now add the lemon juice and a seasoning of salt and freshly milled black pepper.

Pour the soup into a tureen, and if it seems to be a little too thick, thin it slightly with a little cold milk. Now stir in the mint, taste to check the seasoning, cover and chill thoroughly. Serve with the remaining thin slices of cucumber as garnish.

Chilled Curry Soup

For four people the ingredients are:

1 medium onion, chopped
   small
1 medium carrot, chopped
   small
3 oz butter
3 tablespoons flour
Curry powder

2 pints chicken stock (can be
   made from a cube)
1 dessertspoon apricot jam
5-oz carton double cream
A few very small cauliflower
   florets for garnishing
Salt and pepper

Soften the onion and carrot gently in the butter for 10 minutes. Stir in the flour and 1 tablespoon curry powder, then slowly add the stock (see p. 12), a little at a time, stirring well after each addition. Now put a lid on, and simmer gently for 30 minutes, then either sieve the soup or blend it in a liquidizer.

When it has completely cooled, chill it thoroughly in the refrigerator for about 4 hours. Then mix 1 teaspoonful of curry powder with the jam, whip the cream softly, and add the curry and jam mixture to it.

Serve the soup in four individual bowls with a blob of the cream mixture floating in the middle and a sprinkling of raw cauliflower.

Thick Farmhouse Soup

For four people:

½ lb streaky bacon in one piece
3 oz dried yellow split peas
3 oz pearl barley
1 small onion, chopped small
2 leeks, washed and chopped
1 carrot, chopped small

1 small turnip, chopped small
½ small cabbage, shredded
3 pints water
Salt and freshly milled black
   pepper

Place the bacon in a large cooking pot and add the split peas and barley (which should be rinsed in cold water first), then pour in 3 pints of cold water. Add a teaspoonful of salt, bring to simmering point and skim off any scum from the surface. Simmer, with the lid on, for about 1½ hours or until the split peas are soft.

Now take out the bacon, cut off and discard the rind, then chop the meat into smallish pieces and return them to the pot. Next add all the prepared vegetables and some more seasoning, and continue cooking for a further 30 minutes.

Taste to check the seasoning before serving, and serve very hot with wholemeal bread and plenty of butter.

Gazpacho

For six people:

$1\frac{1}{2}$ lb firm ripe tomatoes
4-inch piece cucumber, peeled and finely chopped
2 or 3 spring onions, peeled and finely chopped
$\frac{1}{2}$ large red or green pepper, finely chopped
2 cloves garlic, crushed
4 tablespoons olive oil

$1\frac{1}{2}$ tablespoons wine vinegar
1 heaped teaspoon fresh chopped basil, marjoram or thyme (depending on what is available)
$\frac{1}{2}$ pint cold water
4 ice cubes
Salt and freshly milled black pepper

Start by peeling the tomatoes: place them in a bowl and pour boiling water over them, then, after a minute or two, pour the water away. The skins can now be removed very easily. Now halve the tomatoes, discard the seeds, then chop the flesh roughly.

Next place the tomatoes, cucumber, spring onions and chopped pepper and garlic in a liquidizer, season with salt and freshly milled black pepper, and add the herbs, oil and wine vinegar. Then blend at top speed until the soup is absolutely smooth (if your liquidizer is very small, combine all the ingredients together first, and divide as necessary).

Taste to check the seasoning, and pour the soup into a bowl or tureen, add a little cold water ($\frac{1}{4}-\frac{1}{2}$ pint) to thin it slightly, then cover carefully with foil and chill thoroughly.

Serve the soup with four ice cubes floating in it and a garnish handed round separately – which is made as follows:

$\frac{1}{2}$ large red or green pepper, very finely chopped
4-inch piece cucumber, peeled and finely chopped
2 spring onions, finely chopped

1 hard-boiled egg, finely chopped
1 heaped tablespoon fresh chopped parsley

Combine all these ingredients together with a seasoning of salt and freshly milled black pepper, and hand round at the table together with croutons (small cubes of bread fried till crisp in olive oil).

Kitchen Garden Soup

To make enough for eight:

1 lb leeks
5 celery stalks (approx. ¾ lb)
¾ lb carrots
¾ lb courgettes
1 huge Spanish onion
4 oz streaky bacon, with rinds removed
2 level tablespoons butter
2 level tablespoons oil

1 large or 2 small cloves garlic
3 pints chicken stock (from cubes)
1 heaped tablespoon tomato purée
4 tablespoons fresh chopped parsley
Salt and freshly milled black pepper

Start by preparing the vegetables – trim the leeks, slice them lengthways and then into ¾-inch slices (using the green part as well). Wash them thoroughly, then drain in a colander; next the celery, which should be cut into ¼-inch slices, and the same with the carrots and courgettes. The onion and the bacon should be chopped small.

In the largest saucepan you have, melt the butter with the oil, add the bacon and cook it a little. Then add all the vegetables and the crushed garlic, stir to get everything nice and buttery, and cook over a low heat for 20 minutes stirring now and then.

Finally pour in the stock, taste and season with salt and pepper, then simmer very gently (uncovered) for 2 hours. Just before serving stir in the tomato purée and fresh chopped parsley.

Leek, Onion and Potato Soup

Quantities for four people:

4 large leeks
2 medium-sized potatoes, peeled and diced
1 medium-sized onion, chopped small
1½ pints chicken stock

½ pint milk
2 oz butter
1 tablespoon fresh chopped parsley (if available)
Salt, freshly milled black pepper

To prepare the leeks, discard the tough outer layer and trim the tops and the roots, then split them in half lengthways and slice them quite finely. Now give them a thorough washing in 2 or 3 changes of water to get all the dirt out.

Take a large thick-based saucepan, gently melt the butter in it then add the prepared leeks, potatoes and onion. Stir them all around with a wooden spoon to get them nice and buttery, season with salt and pepper; then, keeping the heat very low, put the lid on and let the vegetables sweat for about 10 minutes.

Add the stock and the milk and bring to simmering point, then replace the lid and let the soup simmer gently for a further 20 minutes or until the vegetables are soft (be careful not to have the heat too high, or it may boil over – because of the milk). Now either press the whole lot through a sieve, or purée in a liquidizer. Return the soup to the saucepan, re-heat gently, taste to check the seasoning, and stir in the parsley just before serving.

Brown Lentil Soup

To serve four to six people:

6 oz brown lentils	8-oz tin Italian tomatoes
6 thick slices streaky bacon, with rinds removed	2 cloves garlic, crushed
2 carrots, sliced	3 pints beef stock (can be made with a cube)
2 onions, halved and sliced	2 tablespoons chopped parsley
2 celery stalks, sliced	Salt and freshly milled black pepper
½ small head cabbage, thinly sliced	

Wash the lentils very thoroughly (it is surprising how many stones and strange looking seeds sometimes lurk amongst them). Now dice the bacon and cook it in a little dripping in a large saucepan until the fat runs. Next add the prepared vegetables and continue to cook, stirring them round now and then until they are lightly coloured. Now stir in the drained lentils plus the contents of the tin of tomatoes, followed by the crushed garlic and beef stock. Bring to the boil, then simmer very gently for 1 hour (with the lid on).

Before serving, taste, season with salt and pepper, and stir in the chopped parsley.

(Note: brown lentils do not require pre-soaking.)

French Onion Soup

Quantities for six people:

2 tablespoons butter
2 tablespoons oil
1½ lb onions, thinly sliced
2 cloves garlic, crushed
½ teaspoon granulated sugar
2 pints good beef stock
½ pint dry white wine
6 slices French bread
8 oz grated Gruyère cheese
Salt and freshly milled black pepper

Heat the butter and oil together in a large saucepan. Stir in the sliced onions, garlic and sugar and cook over a fairly low heat for about 30 minutes, or until the base of the pan is covered with a nutty brown, caramelized film (this browning process is important as it helps the colour of the resulting soup, and also helps considerably with the flavour). Now pour on the stock and wine, bring the soup to the boil, cover and simmer gently for about an hour.

Then taste and season the soup with salt and freshly milled black pepper (and if you really need a stomach-warmer add a tablespoon or two of brandy). Now toast the slices of French bread and spread them with butter. Place each slice in a fireproof soup bowl, ladle the soup on top, and when the toast surfaces sprinkle grated Gruyère cheese over the surface of each bowl. Grill until golden-brown and bubbling.

Green Pea Soup

For four people:

2 lb fresh peas, shelled
4 spring onions, finely chopped
4 lettuce leaves, finely chopped
1 rasher unsmoked bacon, finely chopped
2 oz butter
2 pints hot water
1 tablespoon single cream
1 heaped teaspoon fresh chopped mint
Sugar, salt and pepper

In a large saucepan melt the butter and gently sauté the chopped onion and lettuce and bacon in it for about 5 minutes, then add the peas. Stir around, then pour in the hot water, put on a lid and let the peas simmer gently for about 20 to 25 minutes, or until the peas have cooked. Now press the whole lot through a sieve (the bacon can be discarded), taste to check the seasoning, and re-heat adding a little caster sugar and some fresh chopped mint, and stirring in the cream just before serving. (If you happen to have a couple of fresh spinach leaves handy, these can be chopped and added to the lettuce at the beginning; it will make the soup a lovely dark green colour.)

London Particular

The name was once used to refer to a London 'pea-souper' fog. Ingredients for eight servings:

3½ pints basic stock
¾ lb split peas (yellow or green)
2 oz butter
4 thick rashers bacon, diced
1 medium onion, roughly
   chopped

1 celery stalk, chopped
1 large carrot, sliced
A little extra stock, if needed
Seasoning

First strain off 3½ pints basic stock (see p. 11) into a large saucepan, then bring just up to simmering point, add the split peas, cover and simmer very gently for about 30 minutes (there is no need to soak the split peas first).

Meanwhile, heat 1 oz butter in another saucepan and add the prepared vegetables and the bacon, and cook them over a medium heat until softened and nicely golden – this will take about 15 minutes. Add the softened vegetables to the stock and split peas, season lightly with salt and freshly milled black pepper, then cover and simmer very gently for a further 40 to 50 minutes.

When the soup is ready, either press the whole lot through a sieve or liquidize in an electric blender. Now return it to the saucepan, taste to check the seasoning and add a little more stock if it seems to need thinning a bit.

Before serving, melt the remaining butter into it.

Some crisp fried croutons (fried in bacon fat) would be a nice garnish, and if you want to make the soup into a delicious substantial main course add some chopped cooked frankfurters.

Scallop Soup

For four to six people you need:

4 very large scallops (when taken out of the shells these should weigh approx. ¾ lb)
1 medium onion, chopped small
1 lb potatoes, peeled and diced
2 oz butter
1 pint chicken stock (can be made from a cube)
½ pint milk
2 egg yolks
3 fl. oz double cream
Salt
Freshly milled black pepper

First take a largish saucepan and gently melt the butter in it, add the onion and cook it very gently without letting it colour at all – this will probably take around 10 minutes.

Next add the diced potatoes, stir them into the butter and onions, season with salt and pepper; then, keeping the heat very low, put the lid on and let them sweat for another 10 to 15 minutes. Next pour in the hot chicken stock, stir, then replace the lid and leave to simmer gently for another 10 to 15 minutes.

Meanwhile, you can be preparing the scallops by washing them thoroughly and cutting off the coral-coloured bits – chop them and keep them by on a separate plate. The white parts should be diced roughly, placed in a saucepan with ½ pint milk, together with a little salt and pepper, and poached very gently for 8 to 10 minutes.

When the potatoes are cooked, they and their cooking liquid should be puréed in a blender, or pressed through a nylon sieve.

Now combine the scallops (and the milk they were cooked in) with the potato purée. At this point the pieces of coral roe can be added, and the soup gently heated.

Finally, beat the egg yolks thoroughly with the cream, remove the soup from the heat, stir the egg and cream mixture in and return the pan to a gentle heat, where the soup will thicken slightly – but be very careful not to let it come anywhere near the boil or it will curdle.

To serve, pour the soup into a warm tureen and ladle into warm soup bowls. This really is one of the most delicate and delicious soups imaginable.

(Note: If you want to make this soup in advance, prepare it all except for the cream and egg-yolk bit, which can be done at the last minute just before serving.)

Old English Summer Soup

For four people:

1 smallish cabbage lettuce, washed and shredded
4 or 5 spring onions, finely chopped
2 medium-sized potatoes, finely diced
½ cucumber, chopped

3 oz butter
1½ pints chicken stock (can be made from a cube)
1 bunch fresh snipped chives
Salt and freshly milled black pepper

In a heavy saucepan melt the butter gently, then stir in the potato, spring onions, lettuce and cucumber. Stir everything round in the butter, then, keeping the heat very low, put a lid on and let everything sweat for 10 minutes. Pour in the stock, stir, add some salt and pepper, put the lid on and let it simmer gently for another 20 minutes. Either press the whole lot through a sieve, or purée in an electric liquidizer. Taste to check the seasoning, re-heat and serve with chives stirred in at the last moment. If you like, you can serve this soup chilled – it is delicious either way.

Tomato Soup

Quantities for four people:

1½ lb firm, ripe tomatoes
1 medium onion, chopped small
1 medium potato, chopped small

1 clove garlic
½ pint stock
Basil, olive oil, salt, freshly ground pepper

Gently heat up a little more than 1 tablespoon olive oil in a thick saucepan (a good-quality olive oil is best for this soup), then put the onion, potato and a few chopped basil leaves – or failing that, parsley will do – in to soften slowly without browning. This takes 10 to 15 minutes.

Meanwhile, skin the tomatoes by emptying them into a large bowl and pouring boiling water over them. After a minute or two the skins will slip off very easily.

Now chop the skinned tomatoes roughly, then add them to the potato and onion, giving a good stir with a wooden spoon.

Let them cook for a minute and if you do not happen to have ½ pint good stock to hand, make it by melting half a chicken stock cube in ½ pint hot water and stir in 1 teaspoonful tomato purée.

Next pour the stock over the tomatoes, stir, season with salt, pepper and garlic, then cover and allow to simmer gently for around 25 minutes.

When the soup is ready, pass the whole lot through a sieve to extract the pips. Taste to check the seasoning, and serve with hot crusty French bread and butter.

If the weather is hot, this soup is just as delicious served ice-cold.

Cream of Vegetable Soup

For four good helpings the ingredients are:

1 lb potatoes, peeled and diced	1½ pints chicken stock (from a cube)
3 medium carrots, peeled and sliced	½ pint milk
1 large onion, chopped small	1 tablespoon fresh chopped parsley (if available)
2 leeks, washed and sliced	Salt and pepper
2 oz butter	

Begin by melting the butter in the bottom of a large saucepan, then add all the chopped vegetables and stir well with a wooden spoon to get everything nice and buttery. Season with pepper and salt.

Now, keeping the heat low, put the lid on the saucepan and let the vegetables sweat for about 10 minutes. Next pour in the hot chicken stock and the milk, stir, bring to simmering point, replace the lid and cook for about 25 minutes or until the vegetables are soft. Now either press the whole lot through a sieve or purée in a liquidizer.

Re-heat and taste to check the seasoning before serving, and sprinkle with fresh chopped parsley.

Watercress Soup

For four people:

2 oz butter
6 spring onions, finely chopped.
2 bunches watercress, chopped, washed and dried
2 level tablespoons flour

2 pints chicken stock
2 egg yolks
¼ pint double cream
Salt and freshly milled black pepper

Heat the butter gently in a large saucepan, and cook the chopped onion in it for about 5 minutes until softened but not coloured. Then stir in the watercress, add some salt and pepper, cover the saucepan and let it cook gently for a further 5 minutes, stirring once or twice. Now sprinkle in the flour, and stir over a gentle heat for about 3 minutes, then gradually stir in the hot stock little by little, stirring after each addition.

Now let the soup come slowly to simmering point and simmer (uncovered) for about 5 minutes. Rub the soup through a sieve into a clean saucepan, return to a gentle heat and in a basin combine the egg yolks and cream thoroughly together.

Next whisk a ladleful of hot soup into the cream and egg mixture, then pour this mixture back into the saucepan, whisk again, taste to check the seasoning and, keeping the heat very low, allow the soup to just thicken but *not* come to the boil.

2 Starters

Opinion in this country over 'starters' (for want of a better word) has always been divided. There have been those who have condemned them as excessive luxuries, like Edward III who ordered that 'no man shall cause himself to be served at dinner . . . with more than two courses'. And there have been those, like the famous 17th-century cook Robert May, who thought nothing of serving 'oysters, coller of brawn, pottage of capons, breast of veal, boiled partridge, chine of beef, jegote of mutton and a dish of sweetbreads', all for one first course.

Personally, I like to think of starters simply as appetizers, a little something to tempt the palate to greater things. The nicest starters are nearly always the simplest, and we have in this country some ideal raw materials. Home-grown varieties of tomato such as Ware Cross – which in a tasting experiment I held in the autumn of 1973 came out, according to my panel of professional wine-tasters, tops against its commercial and continental rivals – are perfect in a salad with some vinaigrette with fresh herbs. And it would be hard to beat a few stalks of English asparagus with melted butter.

A visit to Pinney's Smoke-houses in Suffolk in February 1972, confirmed for me that the traditional British art of smoking fish was alive and well – there they specialize in smoking over whole oak chips rather than the sawdust commonly used, and will supply fish by mail order all over the country. But, even for those who want to be more creative over their appetisers, a first course doesn't have to be complicated. With marinading, a humble packet of kipper fillets can be transformed into the smoked salmon class, and impressive soufflés (see pp. 33–34) can be made partly in advance.

Asparagus and Cheese Tart

Quantities for four to six helpings:

for the pastry:
4 oz plain flour
A pinch of salt
1 oz pure lard
1 oz margarine
Cold water

for the filling:
¾ lb asparagus (approx. 15 medium-sized stalks)
2 large fresh eggs
1½ oz grated Cheddar cheese
1 level tablespoon grated Parmesan
½ pint double cream
Salt and freshly milled black pepper

You will need a greased 8-inch round flan tin. Pre-heat the oven to gas mark 4 (350°F), and put a baking sheet in to pre-heat.

First, make the pastry and line the flan tin with it. Prick the base all over with a fork and cook for 10 minutes; remove the pastry and turn the heat up to gas mark 5 (375°F). The asparagus should meanwhile be half-cooked (5 minutes in the steamer), then cut into 1½-inch lengths. Arrange the asparagus evenly over the pastry base, then sprinkle in the Cheddar cheese.

Now whisk the eggs till frothy, and beat them into the cream together with a good seasoning of salt and freshly milled black pepper.

Pour the cream mixture over the asparagus and cheese and sprinkle in the Parmesan.

Place the tart on the pre-heated baking sheet in the oven for about 40 to 45 minutes, until the centre is firm and the filling golden-brown and puffy.

This can be eaten hot or cold. For a slight variation 1 dessert-spoon fresh chopped tarragon can be added to the cream mixture before cooking.

Aubergine Fritters

For four people:

1 lb aubergines

2 tablespoons seasoned flour

Oil for frying

for the sauce

2 oz butter

1½ tablespoons flour

1 tablespoon tomato purée

1 lb fresh ripe tomatoes, peeled and sieved

2 tablespoons white wine

1 teaspoon sugar

2 cloves garlic, crushed

1 tablespoon fresh chopped tarragon (or 1 teaspoon if dried)

1 tablespoon fresh chopped parsley

Salt and freshly milled black pepper

Prepare the aubergines by cutting them lengthwise into ¼-inch thick slices, place them in a colander, sprinkle with salt and leave them for 1 hour to drain with a plate and a heavy weight on top.

Meanwhile, prepare the sauce by melting the butter in a thick saucepan, stirring in the flour and tomato purée, then gradually adding the sieved tomatoes bit by bit to make a smooth sauce. Now add 2 tablespoons white wine, the sugar, garlic, tarragon and a good seasoning of salt and pepper, and simmer gently for 10 minutes, stirring now and then. The aubergines should be dried thoroughly in kitchen paper, dipped in seasoned flour, then deep-fried until golden.

Drain well on crumpled kitchen paper, and serve with the sauce poured over and garnished with chopped parsley. A few deep-fried cubes of bread (croutons) make a nice addition.

Aubergines à la Provençale

For six people:

2 largish aubergines

1 small-to-medium red pepper

1 green pepper (same size)

5 firm, ripe red tomatoes (medium-sized)

1 tablespoon fresh chopped basil

1 fat clove garlic, crushed

1 small onion, finely chopped

Seasoned flour

Olive oil

Salt

Freshly milled black peppeɪ

1 tablespoon fresh chopped parsley

First cut the aubergines lengthwise into ¼-inch thick slices (leaving the skins on), then sprinkle them with salt and leave them for 1 hour to drain in a colander with a plate and a heavy weight on top.

Next, prepare the sauce by heating 2 fl. oz olive oil in a saucepan, and let the chopped onion cook gently in it for 5 or 6 minutes while you de-seed and chop the peppers into smallish strips and peel, de-seed and chop the tomatoes.

Now add the peppers and tomatoes to the onions, together with the crushed garlic and chopped basil. Stir well, add some salt and pepper and let the sauce simmer gently (without a lid) for about half an hour, or until the peppers are tender but still retain their shape – they should not get too mushy.

When the sauce is cooked, taste to check the seasoning. When you are ready to cook the aubergines, dry them thoroughly in some kitchen paper, give each slice a light dusting of seasoned flour, and fry them in hot olive oil till crisp and golden on both sides (you will probably be better off with two frying pans for this, as the aubergines take up a lot of room).

Drain the aubergines on crumpled greaseproof or kitchen paper, and serve them on warm plates sprinkled with chopped parsley, with the sauce handed round separately and lots of warm French bread.

Baked Avocado with Tomatoes and Prawns

For four people:

1 lb small ripe tomatoes	Oil
½ lb peeled prawns, chopped	Freshly milled black pepper
2 medium avocados	Salt
4 tablespoons thick cream	Paprika
1 teaspoon tomato purée	1 tablespoon fresh chopped
½ small onion, chopped small	parsley
1 level teaspoon dried basil	

First pour boiling water over the tomatoes, leave them for about 5 minutes, then peel off the skins and chop the flesh roughly. Now heat a little oil in a thick saucepan and soften the chopped onion in it. Add the tomatoes, basil and tomato purée, stir well and let it all simmer very gently for 20 to 30 minutes without a lid.

Then press the mixture through a sieve or liquidize to a purée.

Stir the cream into the purée and season to taste with freshly milled black pepper and salt. Now peel the avocado and chop the flesh into smallish pieces, then arrange them with the chopped prawns in 4 individual, shallow fireproof dishes.

Pour the tomato and cream mixture over, sprinkle with a little paprika and bake in a pre-heated oven (gas mark 5, 375°F) for 20 to 25 minutes. Serve with paprika and chopped parsley sprinkled over and lots of crusty bread and butter to go with it.

Broccoli Cheese Soufflés

Quantities for six small individual soufflés:

1 lb fresh broccoli	5 fl. oz milk
2 large eggs	1 pinch cayenne pepper
2 extra egg whites	Nutmeg, freshly grated
2 oz Cheddar cheese, grated	Salt and freshly milled black
1 oz butter	pepper
2 level tablespoons flour	A little grated Parmesan cheese

For this recipe you will need 6 individual 4-oz ramekin dishes, well buttered. If you have never made a soufflé before, fear not – it really is not all that difficult. As far as I am concerned, the secret of success lies in the egg whites, which (a) have to be whisked properly, and (b) have to be folded in properly. Once you have mastered (a) and (b), which will be explained in detail, you are home and dry.

First, pre-heat the oven to gas mark 4 (350°F), then take a large meat roasting tin (big enough to hold six soufflé dishes), put about 1½ inches of water in it, and put that in the oven to pre-heat as well. Now, to prepare the broccoli, trim off the very stalky bits, place the rest in a saucepan with a little salt and about 6 fl. oz water, and put the lid on.

Simmer it gently for about 10 to 15 minutes or until the broccoli is soft and most of the water has disappeared. Now drain it well, then transfer it to a large mixing bowl and using a large fork, mash it to a pulp – get it as pulp-like as possible, but do not worry too much about getting rid of all the little fibrous pieces of stalk.

Next, melt 1 oz butter in a saucepan, stir in 2 level tablespoons flour, and when it is smooth gradually add the milk, stirring vigorously after each addition. When all the milk is in you will have a thick glossy paste, and you now mix in the cheese – keeping the pan over a very low heat.

Empty the cheese mixture into the bowl containing the broccoli pulp, and mix everything together very thoroughly. Taste, add a little salt if it needs it, also some freshly milled black pepper, a pinch of cayenne and about ¼ whole nutmeg, freshly grated. Next separate the eggs and add the 2 yolks to the mixture and mix again very thoroughly.

Now, the all-important egg whites – and it may be worth mentioning that all the above can be prepared well in advance (except for pre-heating the oven, which should be about 20 minutes before you need to cook the soufflés). Take a very large mixing bowl, making quite sure it is completely dry and free from grease and a whisk (which must be the same). The best sort of whisk to use is a balloon whisk, but this needs a certain amount of elbow-grease, so if you are not feeling that energetic, a rotary whisk or an electric whisk will do (though it will not give you quite the same volume as a balloon whisk).

Whisk the egg whites until they stand up in peaks when you lift the whisk, but be careful not to over-do it or they will start to flop a bit and go watery. When they are ready, start to add them to the broccoli mixture straight away because beaten egg-whites will not wait. Carefully fold (not stir) them in using a metal tablespoon and turn the bowl round as you fold – adding about a quarter at a time.

Now spoon the mixture into the prepared soufflé dishes, sprinkle a dusting of Parmesan over the tops, place the dishes in the roasting tin, then leave them on a high shelf in the oven for about 25 minutes.

Do not be scared to have a look to see how they are doing – they will not fall flat if you open the oven door. When they are done they should be nicely risen, and beginning to crack on the surface. Do not over-cook them – they should be soft and moist inside – and serve them absolutely immediately.

If you do not get the egg-white bit exactly right and the soufflés fail to rise as much as they should, they will still taste very good. Also if you want to make one large soufflé, use a 1 to 1¼-pint soufflé dish. Sit it in the tin of water as before, pre-heat the oven to gas mark 7 (425°F) and cook it for 30 to 35 minutes.

Chicken Liver Pâté

For two people:

4 oz chicken livers
3 oz butter (at room temperature)
1 tablespoon brandy
1 teaspoon mixed mustard
1 or 2 pinches mixed spice

1 clove garlic, crushed
Salt and freshly milled black pepper
2 tablespoons (approx. 1 oz) melted butter

Take a thick frying pan, melt 1 oz butter in it and fry the chicken livers on a highish heat for about 5 minutes, turning them over frequently.

Then remove them from the pan with a draining spoon and either purée them in an electric blender or press them through a nylon sieve. Pour the brandy on to the juices left in the frying pan (to sort of rinse it out), and pour it over the puréed liver.

Now mix in the rest of the butter, mustard, mixed spice and garlic, then season well with freshly milled black pepper and salt.

Press the whole lot into an earthenware pot, pour the melted butter over it, leave to cool, then cover with foil. Leave it in the bottom of the refrigerator for a day or two. Serve with hot toast and sprigs of watercress.

Country Pâté

Quantities for twelve servings:

1 lb minced beef
1 lb fat belly pork, minced
½ lb pigs liver, minced
4 tablespoons dry white wine
2 tablespoons brandy

2 cloves garlic
6 black peppercorns
6 juniper berries
6 oz fat streaky bacon
1 level teaspoon salt

Two hours before cooking the pâté, mix the minced meats thoroughly in a large bowl and add half the streaky bacon (cut up fairly small).

Mix the bacon in with the salt, then add the peppercorns, garlic and juniper berries (which you should crush by pressing with the back of a tablespoon; or you could use a mortar and pestle).

Pour the wine and brandy over, then leave it in a cool place for 2 hours to soak up all the flavours. Before cooking, pre-heat the oven to gas mark 2 (300°F). Pack the mixture into a large loaf tin, arranging the remaining slices of bacon, cut into strips, on top. Put the loaf tin into a meat-roasting tin filled with water and bake it for about 1½ hours. By the time it is cooked, the pâté will have shrunk quite a bit. Let it cool, without draining off any of the fat. Serve it cut into thick slices.

Courgette Soufflé

For six people as a starter (or four as a main course):

4 oz courgettes, thinly sliced	½ pint milk
5 tablespoons butter	5 egg yolks
2 tablespoons finely chopped parsley	2 oz Gruyère cheese, grated
	1 oz Parmesan, grated
2 teaspoons finely chopped chives	Freshly grated nutmeg
	6 egg whites
½ teaspoon dried oregano	Salt and freshly milled black pepper
3 tablespoons flour	

Pre-heat the oven to gas mark 6 (400°F), and grease a 2½-pint soufflé dish.

Cook the courgettes gently in 2 tablespoons butter until soft and golden, then season and leave them to cool. Sprinkle them with the parsley, chives and oregano, mix well and set aside until needed. Now melt the remaining butter in a saucepan and blend in the flour.

Cook for a few minutes before gradually adding the milk, stirring all the time. Bring to the boil (stirring) then simmer for 2 to 3 minutes. Now cool the sauce (by sitting the base of the pan in some cold water) then gradually beat in the egg yolks followed by the cheeses. Season with salt, pepper and nutmeg. Beat the egg whites until they are stiff and carefully fold them into the cheese mixture. Spoon half the soufflé mixture into the prepared dish, cover with the courgette slices, then pour in the remaining soufflé mixture. Place the dish in a roasting tin and pour boiling water into the tin (to a depth of 1 inch). Put it immediately into the oven and lower the heat to gas mark 3 (325°F).

Bake for 40 minutes, then increase the heat to gas mark 6 (400°F) and bake for further 10 to 15 minutes or until a skewer inserted into the centre of the soufflé comes out clean.

Guacamole

To make four servings:

2 ripe avocados (medium sized)
1 garlic clove, crushed
Juice of ½ medium-sized lemon
½ medium onion, grated
2 large tomatoes
½ teaspoon chilli powder
A dash of tabasco sauce
Salt, freshly milled black pepper

First put the tomatoes in a small basin and pour boiling water over them. Leave them for about 5 minutes and then the skins will slip off very easily. Quarter them, scoop out (and discard) the seeds, then chop the tomatoes into fairly small pieces.

The avocados should be halved, their stones removed, then placed skin-side up on a chopping board. Using your sharpest knife, make an incision down the centre of the skin of each avocado half, then simply peel off the skins (but keep them by). Chop the avocado flesh and put it into a largish mixing bowl together with the lemon juice.

Now, using a teaspoon, scrape the avocado skins to extract all the very green flesh that clings to them (this helps to make the guacamole a really good green colour). Next take a large fork and quickly mash the avocado flesh almost to a purée – a few little lumps do not matter, it is supposed to be like that.

Now add the tomatoes, garlic and onion plus a seasoning of salt and freshly milled black pepper and, finally, the chilli powder and tabasco. Taste to check the seasoning – I always find that it needs quite a bit of salt to bring out the flavour, and if you like you can add a spot more chilli powder.

Cover the bowl with Cellophane and keep it in the lowest part of the refrigerator (or a cool place) until needed. Serve in individual dishes, either with chunks of hot crusty bread or thin slices of toast; and if you want to, you can decorate it with a few black olives and some fresh chopped parsley.

(Note: Guacamole should not be made too far in advance, because the avocado tends to discolour. If this does happen, just give it all a good stir – the flavour will not be affected.)

Herring and Apple Salad

For four people you need:

4 slices pumpernickel bread
4 pickled herrings
4 thin slices Spanish onion
4 slices dessert apple (cores taken out but skins left on), tossed in a little lemon juice

5-fl. oz carton soured cream
1 huge pickled cucumber (from any good delicatessen)
Paprika

Simply lay a slice of onion on each slice of bread, next a slice of apple, then the herring folded in three. Now a dollop of soured cream on each one, then a sprinkling of paprika, and finally some slices of pickled cucumber (which you should first slice into rounds). It will then look as good as it tastes.

Marinaded Kipper Fillets

For four people you will require:

8 kipper fillets, skinned (you can use frozen ones, thawed but not cooked)
1 Spanish onion, thinly sliced
1 bay leaf

For the marinade, mix together:
1 tablespoon lemon juice
1 teaspoon sugar
¼ pint olive oil

Lay the skinned kipper fillets in the bottom of a large shallow china dish, so that they do not overlap each other. Cover the fillets with thinly sliced onion rings, add the bay leaf, then pour the marinade all over. Cover the dish with a lid or, failing that, a double sheet of foil sealed all round the edges. Leave them to marinade in the lowest part of the refrigerator for a minimum of 24 hours.

Serve garnished with lemon slices and watercress, with some thinly sliced brown bread and butter and freshly milled pepper.

Kipper Pâté

To serve six people:

10-oz packet frozen kipper
  fillets, cooked, drained and
  skinned, or 10 oz fresh-
  cooked kippers, skinned
½ small onion, very finely
  chopped
1½ tablespoons fresh chopped
  parsley

4 oz butter (at room
  temperature)
1 lemon
Freshly grated nutmeg
A pinch of cayenne pepper
Salt and freshly milled black
  pepper
Watercress (for garnishing)

Put the kippers into a mixing bowl, add the juice of half the
lemon, then mash them to a pulp using a large fork. Now work
in the butter a little at a time. When all the butter is in and you
have a smooth pulp, mix in the parsley, onion, a good grating of
nutmeg and a pinch of cayenne pepper. Taste the mixture and if
necessary add freshly milled black pepper and a little salt.

Divide the mixture and press into six individual dishes and
garnish with watercress. Serve with lemon wedges to squeeze
over and hot toast.

Quiche Lorraine

Quantities for four to six people:

4 oz plain flour, sieved
Pinch of salt
1 oz margarine
1 oz lard
Cold water

6 thin rashers streaky bacon
  (smoked or green)
½ pint double cream
2 large eggs
Salt and freshly milled black
  pepper

You will need an 8-inch flan tin, but if you happen to have one
that is ½ or 1 inch out either way, it will not matter if the finished
tart is slightly deeper or shallower.

To begin with, grease the flan tin and pre-heat the oven to gas
mark 4 (350°F). Put a baking sheet on to the centre shelf to pre-
heat as well – this baking sheet is essential because it helps the
pastry base to cook through.

Now, quickly make the pastry and roll it out fairly thinly. Line
the flan tin with the pastry, pressing it firmly down and well into

the corner. Prick the base all over with a fork, and pre-bake for 10 minutes, then remove and turn the heat up to gas mark 5 (375°F).

For the filling, gently fry the bacon for a few minutes to melt off a little of the fat, then arrange the rashers over the pastry. Next, thoroughly beat the eggs – a rotary whisk or electric mixer will do this in seconds – and beat in the cream till it is all completely blended. Add some freshly milled black pepper now and very little salt, not forgetting the bacon is already salty.

Pour the mixture over the bacon. Place the tart on the hot baking sheet and leave it to cook for 30 to 40 minutes. It is cooked when the filling is golden-brown and puffy, or, if when you touch the centre gently, it feels firm and set.

If you can serve it while still puffy, so much the better. If you are forced to make it in advance, it will not mind hanging about a bit – it is delicious cold and never suffers from being gently re-heated.

I have served this either as a first course on its own, or as a light luncheon dish with an interesting salad. Once you have mastered a basic quiche, you can experiment with various alternatives: for instance, a little sautéed onion with the bacon. Leeks or spring onions with cream are an inspired combination, and the same might be said for slivers of Gruyère or mild grated Cheddar with onion or bacon, or both.

Rillettes de Tours

Quantities for four:

2 lb piece belly pork (ask the butcher to remove the rind and bones for you)	6 black peppercorns
	6 juniper berries
½ lb back pork fat	2 cloves garlic
1 small glass dry white wine	1 heaped teaspoon fresh thyme (if possible, not dried)
¼ teaspoon powdered mace	Salt

Pre-heat the oven to gas mark 1 (290°F).

Start by taking your sharpest knife and cutting the pork lengthwise into long strips about 1 inch wide. Now cut each strip across into smaller strips, and place these in an earthenware terrine. Cut the fat into small pieces as well and mix these in. While cooking, the extra fat helps to keep the pork properly moist.

When all the meat is chopped, add the thyme, with the peppercorns and juniper berries coarsely crushed (either in a mortar or with the back of a tablespoon). Add salt, about 1 heaped teaspoon, then pour in the wine, together with the garlic and mace.

Mix everything around to distribute all the flavours evenly, put the lid on the casserole, place in the centre of the oven and leave it there for 4 hours. When the time is up, taste a piece of pork and add more salt and pepper if necessary.

Now empty everything into a large fine-meshed sieve standing over a bowl, and let all the fat drip through (press the meat gently to extract the fat).

Take two forks and pull the meat into shreds – some people prefer to pound the meat to a paste, but personally I think it is worth persevering with the fork method, which is how they do it in France. Now pack the rillettes lightly into an earthenware terrine (avoid pressing down too hard). Pour a little of the strained fat over, and keep in a cool place.

Serve with hot toast, or chunks of fresh French bread.

Scallops in the Shell

To serve four:

8 small or 4 large scallops (ask the fishmonger for 4 deep shells)	1½ oz flour
½ onion, chopped small	¼ pint double cream
¼ lb mushrooms, sliced	2 level tablespoons breadcrumbs
2 oz butter	A little extra butter
½ pint dry white wine (a Loire wine would be nice, e.g. Muscadet or Sancerre)	Salt
	Freshly ground black pepper

Begin by slicing the white parts of the scallops into rounds, reserving the coral parts for later, and poach the white slices very, very gently in white wine for about 10 minutes or until tender (scallops should always be cooked very gently or they can turn out tough). When they are cooked, strain them and reserve the liquid.

Melt the butter in a saucepan and gently fry the onion and mushrooms for approximately 15 minutes. Now stir in the flour, then start adding the scallop liquid bit by bit, stirring all the time until you have a thick smooth sauce.

Taste it and add seasoning of pepper and salt as required. Add a bit more butter to the sauce and cook over a low heat for about 6 minutes.

Now take the saucepan off the heat and stir in the white bits of scallop – and the coral pieces as well – then stir in the cream. Return the saucepan to a very gentle flame and heat the mixture through, being careful not to let it reach boiling point.

Divide the mixture into the buttered scallop shells, sprinkle the breadcrumbs over, dot with flecks of butter and brown under the grill for a few minutes.

Serve with crusty French bread and lots of Normandy butter. If you like, you can prepare all this in advance and just put the shells under the grill at the last moment.

Smoked Fish Pâté

Quantities for six to eight people:

1 medium-sized smoked trout	1 tablespoon finely chopped
1 medium-sized smoked buckling	raw onion
	½ lb butter
¼ lb smoked eel	1 lemon
¼ lb smoked salmon (the smaller, cheaper scraps are perfectly good)	Nutmeg
	Salt and pepper

The smoked fish you need for this recipe can be varied as much as you like (kipper, mackerel, etc.)

To make the pâté, skin the fish and take all the flesh from the bones – this is a much simpler operation than it sounds. Put the fish in a large mixing bowl, and chop the smoked salmon very small (chop it the same way as you would chop parsley, in minute bits). Add it to the other fish, then, with a large fork, mash like mad until you have a reasonably smooth paste.

At this point I like to add about 1 level tablespoon very finely chopped raw onion, but this is optional. Next, blend the whole lot with ½ lb softened butter, add the juice of a small lemon and about ¼ whole nutmeg, freshly grated (not ready-ground nutmeg, which has only half the flavour).

Finally, a little salt and freshly ground black pepper – and taste a bit to get the seasoning right. Pack it into a dish or terrine, cover it well and chill lightly (an hour or two).

Serve with baked croutons or hot toast, lemon quarters to squeeze over, and sprigs of watercress to make it look pretty.

Whitebait

For four people you need:

1 lb whitebait	Salt and pepper
2 tablespoons seasoned flour	Cayenne pepper
Cooking oil	1 lemon

Have a large bowl ready with 2 tablespoons seasoned flour in it, then half fill a deep frying pan with oil (a chip pan and basket are ideal for this operation). The oil should be heated to about 380°F, but if you don't have a cooking thermometer, test the heat by throwing in a small cube of bread – if it turns crisp and golden in a couple of minutes, all is well.

While the oil is heating, you should have the oven warm and in it a serving dish with some crumpled kitchen paper on it. Now rinse the whitebait in salted water (the easiest way to do this is put the fish in a sieve and dip the sieve in the water). Shake to remove the surplus moisture and throw the whitebait into a clean cloth. Dry a bit, then toss them in the seasoned flour very thoroughly so that each one gets a good coating.

Test the oil temperature, then place about a quarter of the fish in the chip basket and plunge them in the hot fat and fry them for about 3 minutes. Lift them out and shake the basket a couple of times during the cooking to stop them clinging together. When cooked they should be a very pale gold colour – not too brown.

Shake off any surplus oil and keep them on the heated serving dish to drain. Now do the same with the next quarter, and so on till all are cooked. Don't be tempted to cut corners and throw them all in at once; the water content of the fish will cause violent frothing, the temperature of the oil will be immediately reduced and your lovely whitebait will turn all soggy.

To serve, pull out the kitchen paper, sprinkle the fish with salt and a little cayenne pepper; then dish them on to hot plates and give each person a lemon quarter and some thinly sliced brown bread and butter to go with them.

3 Egg and Cheese Dishes

Time and again, I have come back in the *Evening Standard* to my fresh egg campaign. For years the British housewife has often had to put up with stale eggs, and one of the frustrations of shopping was that there was simply no way of telling just how long they had been sitting on the shelf. But, one thing we can thank the EEC for is the ruling that all egg-boxes must be date-stamped – so now, all we have to do is struggle with the terminology! My first encounter with a box stamped 'Week 34' had me counting on fingers and trying to remember which months had five weeks and which had four.

There is no question that, like everything else, really fresh eggs are superior in flavour and texture. The way to tell if an egg is fresh is to place it in a bowl of cold water: if it sits in a horizontal position on the bottom, it is fresh; if it tilts into a semi-horizontal position, it is not quite so fresh; and if it stands up vertically, it is stale. Only if there is a hairline crack in the shell will this method let you down. But, as soon as you break an egg on to a flat surface, you will be able to tell immediately: a fresh egg will have a double ring of white which can be seen quite clearly and the yolk will be plump and rounded; a stale egg, on the other hand, will look watery and spread itself out and the yolk will look flat.

Although the price of eggs has risen faster than almost anything else, they are still one of the cheapest sources of protein available to us. Combined sometimes with cheese, they can provide the quickest of filling and substantial meals.

Alpine Eggs

To serve three people:

6 large fresh eggs
¾ lb grated Cheddar (or
   Lancashire) cheese
Salt and freshly milled black
   pepper

1 oz (approx.) butter
1 dessertspoon fresh-snipped
   chives (if available)

Pre-heat the oven to gas mark 4 (350°F).

Butter a shallow oval baking dish quite generously, then cover
the base with half the grated cheese. Now carefully break 6 eggs
on to the cheese, season well with salt and freshly milled black
pepper, then sprinkle the rest of the cheese over the eggs, covering
them completely.

Dot with a few flecks of butter here and there, then bake in
the centre of the oven for 15 minutes, by which time the cheese
will be melted and bubbling, and the eggs just set. Just before
serving, sprinkle the chives over, and serve with crusty fresh
bread and a crisp green salad.

For a special occasion serve as a first course, using individual
dishes (buttered) with 1 egg per person and 2 oz grated Gruyère
cheese per person. Prepare and cook in exactly the same way as
above.

Cauliflower, Egg and Celery Cheese

For two people:

1 head of English celery
1 cauliflower
2 hard-boiled eggs
¼ lb mushrooms, sliced
1 large onion
2 oz butter
2 oz flour
½ pint milk

3 oz Cheddar cheese, grated
1 tablespoon dried
   breadcrumbs
1 bay leaf
Nutmeg
Salt and freshly milled black
   pepper

Pre-heat the oven gas mark 7 (425°F). Scrub and chop the celery
and cook it in a little boiling salted water for about 20 minutes.

The cauliflower needs to be trimmed, washed and sat in ¼ pint boiling salted water, together with a bay leaf, for about 10 to 15 minutes with the lid on the saucepan (it should be tender but still firm).

When the cauliflower is ready, drain it – reserving the water – then chop it roughly and arrange the pieces in a buttered fireproof dish along with the celery, sliced mushrooms and hard-boiled eggs (quartered).

Now make the sauce by gently cooking the chopped onion in butter for about 10 minutes, then stir in the flour and add the milk bit by bit, stirring all the time.

When all the milk is in, add the cauliflower water in the same way till you have a smooth sauce.

Taste it now, add salt and pepper and about ¼ whole nutmeg grated. Pour the sauce over the vegetables, sprinkle the grated cheese over, then the breadcrumbs, dot with flecks of butter and bake on a high shelf for 10 minutes until the cheese has browned and melted.

Cheese Soufflé

For three or four people you need:

3 oz grated cheese (any hard cheese can be used, but a mixture of Gruyère and Parmesan is especially good)	1 oz butter
	¼ pint milk
	A pinch of cayenne pepper
3 large eggs, separated	¼ teaspoon dried mustard
1 oz plain flour	A few gratings of nutmeg
	Salt and pepper

Pre-heat the oven to gas mark 5 (375°F). You will need a 1½-pint soufflé dish (or a pie dish would do), well buttered.

First take a medium-sized saucepan, melt the butter, add the flour and stir it over a medium heat for 2 minutes. Now add the milk gradually, stirring all the time, then simmer gently for 3 minutes (still stirring now and then). Next stir in the seasonings and allow the sauce to cool a bit before stirring in the grated cheese, followed by the egg yolks – which should be beaten in quite thoroughly. Now whisk the egg whites till stiff, beat a couple of dollops into the sauce, then fold in the rest very carefully. Pile the mixture into the soufflé dish, place it on a baking sheet in the centre of the oven for about 30 to 35 minutes.

To test if the soufflé is cooked, push a skewer into the centre – if it comes out clean, the soufflé is cooked.

Curried Eggs

For two people:

4 eggs
4 oz long-grain rice

for the curry sauce:

1½ oz butter	1 large onion, peeled and sliced
1 level tablespoon flour	1 teaspoon brown sugar
¾ pint chicken stock (made from a cube)	1 level dessertspoon (or to taste) Madras curry powder
1 small cooking apple, peeled and chopped small	Juice of ½ lemon
	Salt and pepper

Melt the butter and cook the onion in it till soft (about 10 minutes) then add the chopped apple and cook that for 10 minutes or thereabouts. Now stir in the lemon juice and sugar, then the flour and curry powder. Season with pepper and salt.

Add the hot stock gradually, stirring well after each addition to prevent lumps. When all the stock is in, turn the heat very low and allow the sauce to cook for another 10 minutes or so.

Meanwhile, boil 4 eggs, by putting them in cold water, bringing them to the boil, then giving them another 6 minutes after the water reaches boiling point. Peel them under a cold, running tap, and pop them in the hot sauce for a few minutes. Serve with boiled rice and mango chutney.

Florentine Eggs

For two people:

8-oz packet frozen chopped
    spinach, cooked (or the
    equivalent fresh cooked
    spinach), well drained
4 large fresh eggs
1 oz plain flour
1½ oz butter
½ pint milk

2 tablespoons double cream
3 oz grated Cheddar cheese
1 oz grated Parmesan cheese
Freshly milled black pepper
Salt
Nutmeg
A little extra butter

Pre-heat the oven to gas mark 4 (350° F).

Butter a shallow baking dish generously, arrange the cooked
spinach over the base, season with pepper, a little salt and freshly
grated nutmeg, then sprinkle a tablespoon of cream over and put
the dish in the lower part of the oven to heat through.

Melt 1½ oz butter in a thick saucepan, stir in the flour and in-
corporate the milk bit by bit to make a smooth white sauce.

Stir in the grated Cheddar cheese and cook the sauce for 5
minutes over a very gentle heat (stirring now and then).

Now take the baking dish out of the oven, make four depressions
in the spinach and gently break an egg into each one (I like
to sprinkle just a little salt and pepper on to the yolks), then
carefully pour the cheese sauce over to cover everything completely, sprinkle with Parmesan, add a few flecks of butter here
and there, and bake on a high shelf in the oven for 15 minutes.

Eggs Mornay

For two people:

4 large eggs
1 small onion, chopped small
2 oz butter
1 oz flour
½ pint milk

3 oz grated Cheddar cheese
2 tablespoons cream
Salt and freshly milled black
    pepper
Cayenne pepper

First melt 1½ oz butter in a smallish saucepan and gently soften
the onion in it for 10 minutes, then stir in the flour, cook for a

minute or two and then add the milk a little at a time, stirring after each addition to make a smooth creamy sauce.

Season the sauce and let it cook for 5 minutes over a very gentle heat while you boil the eggs. Place the eggs in cold water and, when they reach simmering point, simmer for 6 minutes, then cool them a little under cold running water.

Now add two-thirds of the grated cheese to the sauce. Stir it in and allow it to melt, then finally stir in the remaining $\frac{1}{2}$ oz butter and the cream. Season if needed with salt and freshly milled pepper.

Peel the eggs, halve them, put a layer of sauce in a buttered gratin dish and arrange the eggs (rounded side up) on top. Cover with the remaining sauce, sprinkle the rest of the grated cheese over, and a little cayenne pepper, and place the dish under a hot grill until the cheese and the sauce are bubbling nicely. Serve at once.

Gnocchi

For three or four people:

½ pint milk
5 oz semolina
Nutmeg, freshly grated
3 oz butter

5 oz freshly grated Parmesan
2 eggs, beaten
Salt and freshly milled black
    pepper

Place the milk with the semolina, a little salt and pepper, grated nutmeg and ½ pint water in a saucepan and bring to the boil stirring all the time. Let the mixture boil for about 4 minutes, still stirring, until it is thick enough to stand a spoon up in, then remove from the heat, beat in 1 oz butter, 3 oz grated Parmesan and the beaten eggs. Check the seasoning then spread the mixture in a buttered Swiss-roll tin (approx. 11 × 7 in.). Leave to cool or refrigerate overnight if possible.

Pre-heat the oven to gas mark 6 (400°F). Turn the mixture out, all in one piece, on to a working surface, then using a 1¼–1½ inch plain round cutter, cut out rounds of the semolina mixture. Place the rounds overlapping in a shallow buttered baking dish (using the trimmings, you should get about 30). Dot the top of the gnocchi with the remaining 2 oz butter and bake for 10 minutes. Baste them with the melted butter and sprinkle the remaining 2 oz Parmesan over. Replace the dish near the top of the oven and bake for a further 30 minutes, or until the whole thing is golden brown and bubbling.

Oeufs en Cocotte

For a first course for four people:

4 large eggs
4 tablespoons double cream

Salt and pepper

Butter 4 cocotte dishes generously and place them in the frying pan, with enough water to come about half-way up the sides of the dishes.

Bring the water to boil, then break 1 egg into each dish.

Season with salt and freshly milled black pepper, cover the pan and simmer very gently for 2 minutes.

Then remove the lid and pour a little cream – about 1 table-spoonful – on to each egg. Now replace the lid and continue to simmer for another 2 minutes. Serve immediately with thinly sliced brown bread and butter.

Omelette Savoyard

The ingredients for two are:

4 large eggs
1 large onion, chopped
3 rashers bacon, chopped roughly (but not too small)
2 medium-sized cooked potatoes, chopped

2 oz Gruyère cheese, cut with a small sharp knife into thin slivers
A little butter and oil
Salt and freshly milled black pepper

Start by melting a little butter and oil in a medium-sized frying pan, then gently cook the onions and bacon for 10 minutes. Next, add the chopped potatoes and let them colour a bit for 5 minutes or so, stirring them round the pan. Now turn on the grill to high.

Arrange the slivers of cheese over the other ingredients, beat the eggs with a fork (not too much), season them with freshly milled black pepper and just a little salt.

Turn the heat under the frying pan up to its highest and pour the eggs in, using a palette knife to draw the outside of the omelette in, allowing the liquid egg to escape round the edges. Then place the pan under the hot grill for the top to set. Serve the omelette flat, cut in wedges – do not attempt to fold it.

Piperade

For two people:

- 2 green peppers (de-seeded and cut into strips)
- 1 large (16 oz) tin Italian tomatoes, well drained
- 2 medium onions, chopped small
- 1 or 2 cloves garlic (according to taste), crushed
- ½ teaspoon dried basil
- Salt and freshly milled black pepper
- 4 large fresh eggs
- Butter and olive oil

Melt a knob of butter and a dessertspoon of olive oil in a shallow heavy pan and add the onions. Cook them very gently for 10 minutes without browning.

Now add the crushed garlic cloves, tomatoes and peppers, stir everything round a bit, season with salt, pepper and basil and cook, without covering, for another 20 minutes or so – the peppers should be slightly underdone.

Next, beat the eggs thoroughly, pour them into the pan and, using a wooden spoon, stir exactly as you would for scrambled eggs.

When the mixture starts to thicken and the eggs are almost cooked remove from the heat, continue stirring and serve immediately (as with scrambled eggs, be very careful not to overcook).

Potato and Cheese-baked Eggs

For two people:

- 2 lb potatoes
- 5-oz carton soured cream
- 3 oz butter
- 6 oz Cheddar cheese, grated
- 2 tablespoons grated Parmesan
- Freshly ground black pepper
- Salt
- Freshly grated nutmeg
- 4 large fresh eggs
- A few chopped chives or spring onion tops

Pre-heat the oven to gas mark 5 (375°F).

Peel and cook the potatoes in boiling salted water, then drain them, add the butter and soured cream, start to break the potatoes

up with a fork and then whip them to a cream with an electric mixer.

Now add the cheeses, taste and season with salt, pepper and nutmeg. Next butter a shallow ovenproof dish, spread the potato mixture in the dish, and then with the back of a tablespoon make four depressions. Bake in the oven for 15 minutes, then break the eggs into the little depressions already made, return the dish to the oven, and bake for a further 10 to 15 minutes, or until the eggs are just set.

Serve immediately, sprinkled with chopped chives or spring onion tops.

Tortilla

This particular variety serves two:

4 large eggs
2 potatoes, peeled and diced
1 small green pepper, de-seeded and chopped
1 onion, chopped

2-oz piece Spanish chorizo sausage, cut into smallish dice
3 tablespoons olive oil
Salt and freshly milled black pepper

First, take a medium-sized heavy frying pan and heat 2 tablespoons oil in it, then add the diced potatoes, cooking them gently for about 8 to 10 minutes and stirring them occasionally so that they brown evenly.

Next, add the onion, pepper and chorizo, stir once more and cook for a further 6 to 7 minutes (or until the potatoes are golden brown and the onion soft).

Beat the eggs and season them well, then pour them into the pan, and cook over a medium heat for 2 or 3 minutes – shaking the pan now and then to prevent the eggs sticking.

When the omelette is firm but still slightly moist and the underside is lightly browned, slide it out on to a plate. Quickly heat the other tablespoon of oil in the pan, slide the omelette back into the pan, turning it on its other side, and cook for another 3 minutes. Serve cut into wedges (it must not be folded).

55

4 Fish

As a nation we are supposed not to eat nearly enough fish – particularly since we are surrounded on all sides by waters full of them. Is it because we don't eat enough that so many of our high street fishmongers are disappearing? Or is it because they are disappearing that we don't eat enough fish? Once again, spiralling prices have something to do with it, and I have come across those who tend to believe that meat is now better value – which it actually isn't yet.

When buying fresh fish, beware of fishmongers who carry too much stock. Ideally, a fishmonger should have sold out for the day by mid-afternoon – a well-stocked slab at four o'clock is not a welcome sign. Most fish does freeze perfectly well however, which makes it sometimes cheaper and usually more readily available. It will not have that 'fresh-caught' flavour, but you'll find recipes in this chapter to jazz them up into something rather more interesting.

Baked Fish and Tomato Sauce

For four people the ingredients are:

2½–3 lb tail-piece cod
1 tablespoon butter
1 tablespoon oil
1 Spanish onion, chopped
1 large (16 oz) tin Italian tomatoes
¼ pint dry white wine (or dry cider)

1 level teaspoon dried basil
1 clove garlic, crushed
12 stuffed green olives, sliced
1 pickled gherkin, chopped
Salt
Freshly milled black pepper

Pre-heat the oven to gas mark 6 (400°F).

Wash and dry the fish, then lay it in a buttered baking tin or gratin dish. Next, heat the butter and oil together in a saucepan and gently fry the chopped onion and garlic until softened.

Now add the contents of the tin of tomatoes, 1 teaspoon dried basil and the dry white wine (or cider), then simmer gently (uncovered) for 15 minutes – by which time the sauce should have a jam-like consistency. Stir in the olives and gherkins, taste and season with salt and pepper. Now, pour the sauce over the fish, cover closely with a lid or foil, and bake for 35 to 40 minutes, or until the fish is tender.

This is nice served with buttery creamed potatoes.

Cod Portugaise

For two people:

1 lb thick end cod fillet	6 whole fennel seeds, crushed
1 large onion, chopped	1 tablespoon fresh chopped
1 fairly large green pepper	parsley
1 small (8 oz) tin Italian	Seasoned flour
tomatoes	Olive oil
2 or 3 cloves garlic	Salt and freshly milled black
1 tablespoon lemon juice	pepper

Pre-heat the oven to gas mark 6 (400° F).

Wipe the fish and dry it in kitchen paper. Cut it into 6 or 8 squares, coat them in seasoned flour and fry them in hot olive oil till golden and almost cooked. Transfer them to a casserole, and add a bit more pepper and salt and the lemon juice.

Now, fry the onions and garlic gently for 10 minutes, then add the sliced green pepper and tomatoes and fry for a further 5 or 6 minutes. After that, spoon the lot over the fish, sprinkle the crushed fennel seeds over and bake, without covering, in the oven for 10 minutes.

Serve sprinkled with the fresh chopped parsley. I think plain buttered potatoes are nicest with this.

Fisherman's Pie

To serve four:

1½ lb white fish (fresh haddock
    would be ideal)
1 pint milk
4 oz butter
2 oz plain flour
4 oz peeled prawns
2 hard-boiled eggs, roughly
    chopped
3 tablespoons fresh chopped
    parsley
1 level tablespoon capers
1 tablespoon lemon juice

for the topping:
2 lb freshly cooked potatoes
1 oz butter
¼ pint soured cream
Freshly grated nutmeg

Salt and freshly milled black
    pepper

Pre-heat the oven to gas mark 6 (400°F).

Arrange the fish in a baking tin, season well with salt and pepper, pour ½ pint milk over it and add a few flecks of butter (approx. 1 oz), then bake for 15 to 20 minutes. Pour off and reserve the cooking liquid, then remove the skin from the fish and flake the flesh into largish pieces.

Now, make the sauce by melting the remaining 3 oz butter in a saucepan, then stirring in the flour and gradually adding the fish liquid, stirring well after each addition. When all the liquid is in, finish the sauce by gradually adding the remaining ½ pint milk and seasoning with salt and freshly milled black pepper.

Now mix the fish into the sauce, together with the prawns, hard-boiled eggs, parsley and capers, then taste to see if it needs any more seasoning and stir in the lemon juice. Pour the mixture into a buttered baking dish (about 2½ pints capacity). Next, cream the potatoes starting off with a large fork, then finishing off with an electric beater if you have one, adding the butter and soured cream.

Season the potatoes and add some freshly grated nutmeg, then spread it evenly all over the fish. Bake on a high shelf in the oven (still at gas mark 6, 400°F) for about 30 minutes, by which time it will be heated through and the top will be nicely tinged with brown.

Baked Eggs with Haddock

For three people:

1 lb smoked haddock fillet
½ pint milk (and a little extra)
¼ pint cold water
2 oz butter
2 oz flour
Nutmeg

3 fresh eggs
3 tablespoons grated Cheddar cheese
Salt and freshly milled black pepper

Pre-heat the oven to gas mark 4 (350°F).

Place the haddock in a saucepan or frying pan and pour the milk over, followed by ¼ pint cold water. Now bring slowly to the boil and simmer very gently for about 3 or 4 minutes or until the fish flakes easily when tested with a fork. Take the pan off the heat and remove the fish, reserving the poaching liquor.

Next, flake the fish (discarding any skin or small bones) and arrange it in a shallow, buttered baking dish. Now strain the fish liquor through a sieve into a measuring jug and make it up to ¾ pint with a bit more milk.

Melt the butter in a saucepan and stir in the flour. Cook for about 2 or 3 minutes over a medium heat before gradually stirring in the strained liquor. Now bring to the boil, still stirring, simmer for 2 or 3 minutes, taste and season with salt, pepper and nutmeg (you will need little or no salt).

Pour the sauce over the fish, make three depressions in the mixture with the back of a spoon, and carefully break an egg into each one.

Sprinkle a tablespoon grated cheese over each egg, then bake for 15 minutes until the eggs are just set.

Fresh Haddock with Parsley Cream Sauce

For two people:

1 lb fresh haddock (cut in 2 pieces)	1 oz flour
½ pint milk	3 tablespoons fresh chopped parsley
2 fl. oz fresh cream	1 bay leaf
1 lemon	Salt and pepper
2 oz butter	

Pre-heat the oven to gas mark 4 (350°F).

Wash and dry the fish, then lay it in a baking tin. Season with salt and freshly milled black pepper, and pour the milk over. Put a thin slice of lemon and ½ oz butter on each piece of fish, throw in a bay leaf, then place the tin in the oven. It will take about 20 to 25 minutes to cook and should be basted with the milk every now and then.

When ready, pour off the liquid from the corner of the tin into a jug. Cover the fish and keep it warm. Now in a saucepan melt the remaining 1 oz butter, work in the flour and add the liquid bit by bit to make a smooth creamy white sauce. Taste to check the seasoning and let the sauce cook (covered) over the lowest possible heat for about 10 minutes, then stir in the cream and parsley.

Serve the fish with the sauce poured over and garnished with lemon quarters.

Lemon Stuffed Haddock

Quantities for two people:

¾ to 1 lb fresh haddock (from the thick end)
1 small lemon
1 egg
2 tablespoons freshly chopped parsley
2 oz fresh breadcrumbs
2 oz butter
¼ level teaspoon thyme
Salt
Freshly milled black pepper
A little extra butter
Sprigs of watercress

Pre-heat the oven to gas mark 5 (375°F).

Butter a shallow baking dish quite generously, then divide the haddock into two portions and place them side by side in the dish. Season with salt and freshly milled black pepper.

Now prepare the stuffing by mixing the breadcrumbs, thyme and parsley together, and adding the freshly grated rind of the lemon and a tablespoon of the juice. Season with salt and freshly milled black pepper, then melt the butter in a small saucepan and stir it into the breadcrumb mixture, and finally add a beaten egg to bind it all together. Spread the stuffing all over the haddock, dot with flecks of butter and bake for about 30 to 35 minutes.

Serve garnished with sprigs of watercress and lemon quarters to squeeze over. New potatoes with butter and snipped chives make a nice accompaniment.

Smoked Haddock with Cream and Egg Sauce

For four people:

1½ lb smoked haddock
Salt and freshly milled black pepper
½ pint milk
1 bay leaf
2 oz butter (approx.)
2 level tablespoons flour
1 small onion
3 tablespoons cream (single or double)
1 hard-boiled egg, chopped small

Pre-heat the oven to gas mark 4 (350°F).

Place the fish in a baking tin, season with freshly milled black pepper and a little salt, add a bay leaf, and pour the milk over.

Add a few flecks of butter and bake (without covering) for about 20 minutes.

Meanwhile, chop the onion minutely and sauté it very gently, without browning, in about 1½ oz butter. When the fish is cooked, pour all the liquid into a jug and keep the fish warm.

Now add 2 tablespoons flour to the butter and onion, stir till smooth and add the fish liquid, a little at a time, until you have a smooth sauce.

Cook the sauce on a very low heat for about 6 minutes, then add the chopped hard-boiled egg and the cream to it.

Serve the fish with the sauce poured over. Creamed potatoes and peas are nice with this.

Stuffed Baked Herrings

Quantities for four people:

4 herrings with roes	2 slices white bread (crusts removed)
1 tablespoon butter	
1 small onion, finely chopped	Milk
2 hard-boiled eggs, chopped	1 teaspoon lemon juice
1 clove garlic, crushed	Salt and freshly milled black pepper
3 tablespoons chopped parsley	
¼ teaspoon dried thyme	

Pre-heat the oven to gas mark 5 (375°F).

Have the fishmonger remove the heads from the herrings and then gut and fillet them, if you are not sure how to do this yourself. Make sure you get the roes. Wash the fish and dry it on kitchen paper, then heat the butter in a small saucepan and fry the onion gently for 10 minutes or so until soft. Place the onion in a bowl with the chopped eggs, garlic, parsley and thyme.

Soak the bread in milk, squeeze out the excess and shred pieces of it into the bowl. Chop the herring roes and fold this into the mixture along with the lemon juice and salt and pepper.

Now fill each herring with some of the stuffing, fold them back over to their original shape and lay them in a shallow, buttered baking dish.

Put a good knob of butter on each fish and bake near the top of the oven for 30 to 40 minutes, basting with the buttery juices from time to time. Creamy mashed potatoes, with some sautéed spring onions mixed in, go very well with this.

Herrings Fried in Oatmeal

For this recipe ask the fishmonger to clean and bone out the fish for you, so that they are flat, shaped like kippers. For two people you will need:

4 herrings	1 teaspoon oil
3 tablespoons medium oatmeal	Salt and pepper
1 oz butter	1 lemon

Heat up the oil and butter in a large frying pan and while it's heating, wipe the herrings to remove any excess moisture.

Then coat them in the oatmeal, which should first be seasoned with freshly milled black pepper and salt. Press the oatmeal all over quite firmly, and when the fats are hot and frothy fry the herrings in it for approximately four minutes on each side, until they are crisp and golden.

Drain on crumpled greaseproof paper and serve with wedges of lemon to squeeze over.

Powdered mustard mixed with cream (or top of the milk) goes very well with this, and so do plain boiled potatoes.

Fish Kebabs

Quantities for two people:

1 lb cod (thick end of fillet)	1 medium green pepper, chopped
3 tablespoons olive oil	
1½ tablespoons lemon juice	1 medium onion, quartered
1 tablespoon dry white wine	Salt
2 tablespoons finely chopped parsley	Freshly milled black pepper
	Lemon quarters

First, remove the skin from the cod and cut the fish into 1 in. cubes. In a bowl mix the olive oil, lemon juice, wine and chopped parsley, mixing thoroughly with a fork, then, immerse the cubes of cod in it. Separate the layers of the onion quarters and arrange them all over the cod. Leave it now in a cool place for about an hour.

To cook, pre-heat the grill to high, then thread the pieces of cod on to skewers, alternating with pieces of onion and green pepper, and season. Place the skewers on a foil-lined grill pan, brush with the marinade, then grill for a minute or two.

Reduce the heat to medium and cook the kebabs for 4 to 5 minutes each side, brushing on more of the marinade before turning. Serve with a savoury rice with the juices from the grill pan spooned over, and lemon quarters to squeeze over.

Mackerel with Butter and Spring Onions

For four people:

4 fresh medium-sized mackerel	2 tablespoons fresh chopped parsley
1 tablespoon seasoned flour	1 tablespoon lemon juice
A little butter and cooking oil	1 large lemon, cut into quarters
4 oz butter	
2 tablespoons spring onions, very finely chopped	Salt and freshly milled black pepper

Pre-heat the oven to gas mark 4 (350° F).

Wash the mackerel thoroughly under cold running water and dry in a clean cloth or kitchen paper. Take your sharpest knife and make a slit about 3 inches long right next to the backbone of each mackerel (to form a sort of pocket). Now give each fish a light dusting with seasoned flour and fry them in a fairly hot mixture of butter and oil for about 5 minutes on each side. This should make the outside skins nice and crisp.

Now, spread a sheet of foil around the bottom of a roasting tin and place the mackerel so that the slits in their backs are uppermost. Mix the butter, spring onions, lemon juice, parsley and a seasoning of salt and pepper together in a small basin. Stuff this mixture into the pockets and bake in the oven for 20 to 25 minutes.

Serve the fish with the juices spooned over, and give each person a lemon quarter to squeeze over.

Plaice Fillets with Cheese

For two people the ingredients are:

4 smallish plaice fillets	3 oz melted butter
6 oz stale breadcrumbs	½ lemon, cut into quarters
2 oz grated Cheddar cheese	Salt and freshly milled black
1 tablespoon fresh chopped parsley	pepper

Pre-heat the grill to its highest setting, line the grill pan with foil and paint the foil with melted butter. Melt 3 oz butter in a small saucepan, take it off the heat and mix it with the bread-crumbs, grated cheese and parsley. Lay the plaice fillets on the foil-lined grill pan, season them with salt and freshly milled black pepper, then cover them with the buttered breadcrumbs, add a few more flecks of butter here and there, then place under the hot grill until the crumbs have turned a rich brown.

Serve immediately, garnished with lemon quarters, with sauté potatoes and a crisp green side salad.

Florentine Plaice Fillets

To serve four:

1 lb plaice fillets	*for the cheese sauce:*
8 oz fresh spinach (cooked and drained) or an 8-oz packet frozen chopped spinach (thawed)	2 oz butter
	1½ oz plain flour
	¾ pint milk
1 dessertspoon lemon juice	3 oz grated Cheddar cheese
2 oz grated Cheddar cheese	Salt, freshly milled black
1 heaped teaspoon grated Parmesan	pepper, cayenne pepper
1 tablespoon dried breadcrumbs	
Nutmeg	
Butter, salt, freshly milled black pepper	

Pre-heat the oven to gas mark 6 (400°F).

First, make a cheese sauce by melting 2 oz of butter in a small thick-based saucepan, stirring in 1½ oz of flour and blending with a wooden spoon. Cook for a few minutes, then work in ¾ pint milk, a little at a time, till you have a smooth white sauce. Season with salt and freshly milled black pepper to taste. Now stir in 3 oz grated Cheddar cheese (together with a pinch of cayenne pepper) and allow it to melt while the sauce barely simmers for about 3 minutes.

Butter a wide shallow baking dish generously, cover the base with the chopped spinach (with a little grated nutmeg sprinkled over), then arrange the plaice fillets on top. Season with salt and pepper and lemon juice, then pour the cheese sauce over. Sprinkle on a little more grated nutmeg, followed by the grated Cheddar, the Parmesan and the breadcrumbs. Dot with flecks of butter and bake in the oven for around 20 to 25 minutes, by which time the cheese will be melted and turning brown.

Prawn Curry

For two people:

½ lb peeled prawns
2 oz butter
1 medium onion, chopped
1 level tablespoon flour
1 heaped teaspoon Madras curry powder (or to taste)
½ pint tomato juice
½ lb tomatoes, peeled and chopped
½ cucumber, peeled and diced
1 clove garlic, crushed
1 level teaspoon mango chutney
2 or 3 tablespoons double cream
Salt and freshly milled black pepper

In a medium-sized saucepan melt the butter and sauté the onion and garlic over a low heat until soft (about 10 minutes). Stir in the flour and curry powder and, keeping the heat low, cook for a further 3 or 4 minutes, stirring all the time.

Then, still stirring, gradually add the tomato juice, followed by the chopped tomatoes and diced cucumber. Simmer gently (uncovered) until the cucumber is just tender – about 5 or 6 minutes.

Then add the prawns and chutney, stir in the cream, cook just long enough to heat through; taste and season with salt and freshly milled black pepper. Serve either hot or cold with rice.

Chilled Salmon Loaf

For four people the ingredients are:

1 lb fresh cooked salmon, flaked
4 oz butter (at room temperature)
2 tablespoons mayonnaise
1 small onion, chopped minutely
2 stalks celery, chopped small
2 dessertspoons fresh chopped parsley

1 tablespoon lemon juice
Salt
A pinch or two of cayenne pepper
Crisp lettuce leaves
A few sprigs watercress
2 hard-boiled eggs

In a largish mixing bowl mash the salmon to a pulp with a fork, season with a little salt, two pinches of cayenne and some lemon juice, then work the butter and mayonnaise (see p. 161) into the salmon until you have a smooth paste.

Now add the onion, celery and parsley, mix everything thoroughly, then press the mixture into a loaf tin, cover with foil and chill thoroughly for about 4 hours.

To serve, turn the salmon loaf out on to a bed of crisp lettuce leaves, decorate with sprigs of watercress and slices of hard-boiled egg, and serve with a cucumber salad.

Fresh Salmon Tart

For four to six people:

¾ lb cooked salmon, flaked
8 fl. oz double cream
2 large eggs
Salt
Freshly milled black pepper
Nutmeg

The shortcrust pastry is made with:
4 oz plain flour
1 oz butter
1 oz lard
A pinch of salt
Cold water to mix

A buttered 8-inch round flan tin will be needed. Put a baking sheet in the oven and pre-heat to gas mark 4 (350°F).

First, roll the pastry out and line the flan tin, then prick the base all over with a fork and place it in the oven for 10 minutes to start cooking. Whisk the eggs till frothy, then whisk the cream into them, season with salt and freshly milled black pepper. When the pastry has been in the oven for 10 minutes, remove it and turn the heat up to gas mark 5 (375°F); arrange the flaked salmon all over the base of the tart, and pour in the egg and cream mixture. Sprinkle some freshly grated nutmeg all over the surface, then return the tart to the baking sheet in the oven and let it cook for about 30 to 40 minutes until puffy and golden and the centre is firm to touch. This is best served straight from the oven, but is almost as nice if eaten cold.

Smoked Salmon Quiche

To serve four people:

¼ lb chopped smoked salmon
8 fl. oz double cream
2 eggs
Nutmeg
Salt
Freshly milled black pepper

Shortcrust pastry (made with
    2 oz fat and 4 oz plain flour)

For this recipe you will need an 8-inch flan tin. Pre-heat the oven to gas mark 4 (350°F).

Begin by making the shortcrust pastry and line the tin with it; prick the base all over with a fork and place it in the oven, on a baking sheet, for about 10 minutes to start the pastry off, then remove it and turn the oven up to gas mark 5 (375°F).

Meanwhile, break the eggs into a basin, season with freshly milled pepper and a pinch of salt, then whisk them till frothy.

Now, whisk in the double cream, quite thoroughly. Take the pastry case out of the oven and quickly arrange the pieces of smoked salmon all over the base.

Pour the cream and egg mixture over, sprinkle on a little freshly grated nutmeg, and return the tin to the baking sheet, where it will cook and turn golden brown and puffy in about 25 to 30 minutes – it is done when the centre feels just set.

Chilled Salmon Trout with Cucumber and Tarragon Sauce

For four people:

- 1 salmon trout (weighing about 2 lb)
- 3 oz butter
- 4 inches cucumber, peeled and chopped small
- 1 tablespoon fresh chopped tarragon
- 5-oz carton soured cream
- 1 tablespoon fresh cream or top of the milk
- Salt and freshly milled black pepper

Pre-heat the oven to gas mark $\frac{1}{2}$ (250°F). Make sure you have a large double sheet of foil large enough to wrap the fish completely.

Put 1 oz butter in a saucepan to melt over a low heat and then, using a pastry brush, brush it all over the foil. Lay the cleaned wiped fish on the foil, put 1 oz butter inside the fish and 1 oz butter on top.

Sprinkle with a little salt and freshly milled black pepper, then wrap it loosely but securely, pinching the foil together to seal well. Place the trout in the oven and cook for $1\frac{1}{4}$ hours. Leave the fish inside the foil (without opening it) till needed. To make the sauce, combine the soured cream, tarragon, cucumber and cream; season, cover and chill well before serving.

Skate with Black Butter

Quantities for four people:

- 1 lb skate wings
- 3 tablespoons wine vinegar
- 1 bay leaf
- 1 blade of mace
- A couple of sprigs parsley
- 3 oz butter
- 1 level tablespoon chopped capers
- Salt
- Freshly ground black pepper
- A few lemon slices

Place the skate wings side by side in a large wide pan (or a roasting tin), add pepper and salt, 2 tablespoons wine vinegar, bay leaf, mace and parsley. Add just enough water to cover, then bring slowly to the boil and simmer gently until the fish is cooked

– about 10 to 15 minutes – but it is most important that the fish should not be overcooked.

Meanwhile, slowly melt the butter in a small saucepan, then pour the clear golden butter into another saucepan, leaving the white sediment behind. Now, heat the butter until it is a rich warm brown, then remove immediately from the heat and stir in the remaining vinegar, chopped capers and a seasoning of salt and pepper. Drain the fish thoroughly, discarding the herbs. Arrange it in a heated serving dish, with the butter poured over and garnished with slices of lemon.

Oven-Baked Trout with Cream and Chives

For two people:

2 trout (weighing 7 or 8 oz each)	3 fl. oz double cream
Butter	1 bunch snipped chives

Pre-heat the oven to gas mark 7 (425°F).

Line a roasting tin with buttered foil, place the trout (washed and thoroughly dried) on it, and brush them with a little melted butter. Season with salt and freshly milled black pepper, then bake them on a high shelf in the oven for 10 minutes.

Meanwhile, bring the cream to boiling point in a small saucepan, stir in the chives, a generous lump of butter, some salt and freshly milled black pepper, then pour the sauce into a jug to serve with the fish.

Poached Trout with Herbs

For four people:

4 frozen rainbow trout	4 slices lemon
1 glass dry white wine (or cider)	2 bay leaves
6 black peppercorns	Water
1 teaspoon dried mixed herbs	Salt
½ onion, cut into rings	

If you do not have a frying pan large enough to hold four trout at once use a fairly solid meat roasting tin.

Lay the trout flat in the frying pan, side by side (it does not matter if they are still frozen solid), throw in the peppercorns, onion rings, lemon slices and bay leaves. Then add salt and sprinkle in the herbs. Now pour the wine over and add enough

cold water to just cover the trout. Bring them to simmering point, and keep simmering for 10 to 12 minutes.

Lift the fish out with a slice, allowing the excess liquid to drain off, and serve with melted butter. If the trout have thawed out before you start cooking they will need only 6 minutes simmering time.

5 Meat

Over the period that these recipes appeared in the *Evening Standard*, meat prices were soaring. A Government enquiry team went to Smithfield Market in the freezing dawn, and I remember one butcher urging his customers to 'sell the car, buy a joint'. There were even complaints that butchers were keeping their beef in the safe, and their money in the freezer. But, while they were not generally responsible for soaring costs, the crisis did bring home the importance of finding yourself a good butcher.

The famous cookery-writer Hannah Glass was once supposed to have begun a recipe 'First catch your hare', and I am often tempted to begin my recipes 'First catch your butcher'. An absolute essential for any successful meat dish is a sympathetic butcher. So many people are fickle in their custom, just wandering into the nearest shop or buying meat pre-packed in a supermarket (a much more expensive method). But if you make friends with a good butcher, buy from him regularly, and ask his advice, he will give *you* the best of everything. I couldn't survive in my job without my butcher, who tells me week by week what is at its best and in season, and how prices are.

Seasons play a greater part in meat cooking than is often realized. In June and July English lamb is in its prime season (and said to have the finest flavour in the world at that time). In February, though, New Zealand lamb is better, and remains so until early summer. And while pork is available, and its prices steady, all the year round, beef is at its best in autumn, when there will also be a plentiful supply of useful oxtails, ox kidneys etc. (see chapter 7).

BEEF AND VEAL

Beef Braised in Beer

For four to six people:

2 lb chuck steak, trimmed and
cut into 1½-inch pieces
¾ lb onions, roughly chopped
2 tablespoons beef dripping
1 garlic clove, crushed
½ level teaspoon dried thyme

1 bay leaf
1 rounded tablespoon plain
flour
½ pint pale ale
Salt and freshly milled black
pepper

A largish flameproof casserole is ideal for this – then you can start the cooking on top of the stove and transfer it into the oven to finish. The oven should be pre-heated to gas mark 2 (300°F).

Melt the dripping in the casserole and gently fry the onion and garlic in it for 5 minutes or so, then turn the heat up a bit and add the beef. Start to move the meat around a bit with a wooden spoon to brown it nicely on all sides, then sprinkle in the flour and stir it around to soak up all the juices – don't worry if it looks a bit disastrous at this point, it is supposed to.

Now gradually stir in the pale ale, season with salt and freshly milled black pepper, and throw in a bay leaf and ½ teaspoon thyme. When it reaches simmering point, put the lid on the casserole, transfer it to the middle shelf of the oven and leave it there, undisturbed, for 2½ to 3 hours – the beer needs at least this time to develop into a delicious sauce. Before serving, taste to check the seasoning and serve with Onion Rice (see p. 153) and vegetables.

Braised Steak and Onions

For two people the ingredients are:

1 lb braising steak, cut into four pieces
2 largish onions, halved and sliced
¼ pint beef stock (made from a cube)
4 drops Worcestershire sauce
1 dessertspoon beef dripping
Salt and freshly milled black pepper

Pre-heat the oven to gas mark 3 (325°F).

Melt 1 dessertspoon beef dripping in a frying pan, and when it is fairly hot brown the pieces of meat in it on both sides – they should get to a good brown colour. Transfer them to a casserole, then fry the onions to brown them very slightly.

After that arrange them all over the meat, and season with salt and pepper. Now pour in the hot stock and a few drops of Worcestershire sauce.

Next, put on the lid and leave the casserole in the pre-heated oven for about 2½ hours, or until the meat is tender. If you happen to have ¼ pint red wine to spare, then that would be even nicer to use than the stock.

Serve with creamed potatoes and a green vegetable.

Beef Braised in White Wine

For two people the ingredients are:

1 lb chuck steak, cut into bite-sized cubes
2 medium onions, roughly chopped
1 clove garlic, crushed
1 small sprig fresh thyme (or ¼ teaspoon dried)
1 bay leaf
1 dessertspoon flour
½ pint dry white wine
1 small strip orange peel (about 1 inch)
Oil
Salt and freshly milled black pepper

Pre-heat the oven to gas mark 3 (325°F).

In a flameproof casserole melt a little oil and gently fry the onion and garlic in it for about 10 minutes, then turn the heat up a bit and add the cubes of meat. Using a wooden spoon, keep them on the move until they are nicely browned all over.

Now sprinkle in the flour and let that cook and soak up the juices, then gradually stir in the white wine. Add the herbs and orange peel, season with salt and freshly milled black pepper, bring to simmering point, then put the lid on and let it cook gently in the oven for about 2½ hours, or until the meat is tender. If you like, you can cook this on top of the stove in a thick saucepan, but keep an eye on it and stir now and then to prevent sticking.

Chilli con Carne

Quantities to serve four:

- 1 lb chuck steak, cut into very small pieces
- 2 medium onions, chopped
- 1 fat clove garlic, crushed
- 1 pint hot beef stock
- 2 heaped tablespoons tomato purée
- 1 rounded tablespoon flour
- ½ lb red kidney beans (available from healthfood shops)
- 1 green pepper, de-seeded and chopped
- 1 level teaspoon dried chilli (see below)
- Beef dripping
- Salt and freshly milled black pepper

Chilli con Carne *should* be hot and spicy, and for it you can use fresh chillies, chilli powder or crushed dried chillies. Chilli powder can vary a lot, so if you're not sure about yours, *be sparing* with it. If you're in any doubt or don't like it too hot, use less than 1 teaspoon.

First, cover the beans with cold water, bring them to simmering point, simmer for 2 minutes then let them soak for 1 hour. Towards the end of the soaking time, pre-heat the oven to gas mark 2 (300°F). In a flameproof casserole, melt about 1 tablespoon beef dripping and gently cook the onion and garlic in it for about 6 minutes, then turn the heat up, add the beef and brown it (stirring it and turning it around).

Next, add the flour, stir it in to soak up the juices, then mix the tomato purée with the hot stock and add it gradually to the meat and onion. Add the chilli, then, after draining the red beans thoroughly, add them to the rest. Bring to simmering point, cover and cook for about 1½ hours. Then stir in the chopped peppers, return to the oven and cook for a further 30 minutes.

Goulash

To serve four:

1½ lb chuck steak, trimmed and cut into 1½-inch cubes	1 large (16 oz) tin Italian tomatoes
2 large onions, roughly chopped	1 medium-sized green (or red) pepper
1 garlic clove, crushed	5-oz carton soured cream
2 oz beef dripping	Salt, freshly milled black pepper
1 rounded tablespoon flour	
1 rounded tablespoon paprika	

Pre-heat the oven to gas mark 2 (300° F).

Begin by melting the dripping in a flameproof casserole and gently cooking the onions and garlic in it for about 5 minutes. Now turn up the heat a little, add the cubes of meat and brown them on all sides by stirring them round and turning them over. Now sprinkle in the flour and paprika, have another good stir to soak up all the juices, then pour in the tomatoes. Season with salt and freshly milled black pepper, and as soon as it reaches simmering point put the lid on and place it in the middle shelf of the oven for 2 hours.

Prepare the pepper by halving it, removing the seeds and cutting it into 2-inch strips, then when the 2 hours are up, stir the chopped pepper into the goulash, replace the lid, cook for a further ½ hour. Just before serving, stir in the soured cream to give a marbled, creamy effect, then sprinkle a little more paprika over, and serve straight from the casserole with rice (or vegetables).

Meat Loaf

To serve four:

1¼ lb lean minced beef
¾ lb pork sausage meat
1 small green pepper, finely chopped
1 large Spanish onion, chopped small
3 medium slices bread

1 level teaspoon dried mixed herbs
1 clove garlic, crushed
2 tablespoons milk
1 beaten egg
Salt and pepper

Pre-heat the oven to gas mark 8 (450°F).

In a large mixing bowl blend the beef and the sausage meat thoroughly and add the chopped green pepper, onion, herbs and garlic, and mix again.

Now take the crusts off the bread, soak it in the milk, squeeze the excess milk out and add the bread to the meat; then have another good mix. Season well with salt and freshly milled black pepper, bind it all with a beaten egg and pack it into a medium-sized loaf tin. Bake it for 15 minutes then turn the temperature down to gas mark 3 (325°F) and cook for another 45 minutes or so.

When you first turn the oven on for this, you could also put in some medium-sized jacket potatoes which would then be cooked more or less at the same time; these go particularly well with the meat loaf. Tomato sauce made with tinned tomatoes is a nice accompaniment and, eaten cold, it is delicious with crusty bread and butter and pickles.

Turkish Rissoles

For two people:

½ lb leftover beef (or lamb)
1 small onion
½ red or green pepper
1 thick slice bread (crusts removed)
2 tablespoons milk
¼ level teaspoon ground cinnamon
¼ level teaspoon chilli powder

1 clove garlic, crushed
1 tablespoon fresh chopped parsley
1 beaten egg
Seasoned flour
Fat or oil for frying
Salt and freshly milled black pepper

Pass the meat through the finest blade of the mincer, then squash the onion and the pepper through as well. Now place all the minced ingredients in a mixing bowl, mix them together then add the garlic, cinnamon, chilli powder, parsley and the bread (which should first be soaked in milk, and then have the excess milk squeezed out).

Mix the bread and the rest of the ingredients very thoroughly, add a good seasoning of salt and pepper, and finally add a beaten egg to bind the mixture. Form the mixture into small cake shapes, roll them in seasoned flour, and fry in medium-hot fat for 5 to 6 minutes on each side.

Drain well on crumpled greaseproof paper and serve with Onion Rice (see p. 153) and a dollop of yoghurt (Turkish style) or with Tomato and Chilli sauce.

Tomato and Chilli Sauce

¾ lb red ripe tomatoes, peeled, de-seeded and chopped
1 small onion, finely chopped
1 clove garlic, crushed
1 teaspoon tomato purée
1 dessertspoon fresh chopped basil

¼ teaspoon chilli powder
Olive oil
Salt and freshly milled black pepper

Pour boiling water over the tomatoes, leave them for a minute or two, then put them in cold water and slip the skins off. Halve them now, discard the seeds and chop the flesh quite small.

Heat 1 tablespoon olive oil in a saucepan and add the onion and garlic; when they have softened add the tomatoes, tomato purée, the basil and chilli powder, and season. Stir well, then simmer gently for 15 minutes with the lid on, then for a further 10 or 15 minutes without the lid.

Finally, taste to check the seasoning, then either sieve the mixture or blend it in a liquidizer, or else serve it just as it is. This sauce also goes well with chops or hamburgers.

Four Star Shepherd's Pie

Quantities to serve four people:

for the meat mixture:

1 lb best-quality minced beef	½ teaspoon mixed herbs
1 large carrot, chopped very small	½ teaspoon ground cinnamon
2 medium onions, chopped	1 tablespoon fresh chopped parsley
1 level tablespoon flour	Pepper, salt
½ pint hot beef stock mixed with 1 tablespoon tomato purée	Beef dripping

Fry the onions in dripping till soft, then add the carrot and minced beef and cook for about 10 minutes until the beef is browned nicely. Add salt, pepper, cinnamon, mixed herbs and parsley, then stir in the flour and gradually add the stock and tomato purée. Bring to simmering point, cover and simmer very gently for 45 minutes, stirring now and then to prevent sticking.

for the topping:

2 lb potatoes	2 oz butter
2 medium leeks, chopped	Seasoning

Boil the potatoes in salted water and meanwhile melt the butter and gently cook the chopped leeks in it.

When the potatoes are done, cream and stir in the leeks and butter. Place the meat mixture in the bottom of a well-greased baking dish, spread the potato-and-leek mixture on top and bake in the oven (pre-heated to gas mark 6, 400° F) for about 25 minutes.

Entrecôte Hongroise

For two people you will need:

2 entrecôte steaks (each weighing 6–8 oz)
1 small pepper (green or red)
1 small onion
2 tablespoons soured cream (or ordinary cream if easier)
3 fl. oz red wine
½ teaspoon paprika
Salt and freshly milled black pepper
A little oil and butter

First of all chop the onion and pepper finely, then take a good thick frying pan (about 7–8 in.) and cook the onion and pepper in a little butter and oil to soften. Then remove them and keep on one side. Now turn the heat up and get the pan as hot as you dare, then sear the steaks – which should be seasoned with freshly milled black pepper – on one side.

Turn them over and, while the other side is searing, spoon the onion and pepper on top of both steaks. When they are almost cooked to your liking (6 or 7 minutes for a medium-rare steak), pour the wine into the pan, let it bubble and reduce, then add the cream, paprika and a little salt and let it bubble a bit more.

The sauce should be syrupy and not too liquid. Serve the steaks with the sauce poured over.

Steak au Poivre

For two people:

2 entrecôte (or sirloin) steaks (each 6–8 oz)
2 heaped teaspoons whole black peppercorns
2 tablespoons olive oil
½-glass red wine
Salt

Crush the peppercorns very coarsely with the back of a tablespoon (or a pestle and mortar), then coat each steak with olive oil and press the crushed peppercorns on to both sides of each steak.

Pre-heat a thick-based frying pan, without any fat in it, and when it is very hot sear the steaks quickly on both sides.

Then reduce the heat and finish cooking them according to how you like them (a medium-rare entrecôte will take about 6 or 7 minutes and should be turned several times during the cooking).

One minute before the end pour in the wine, let it bubble, reduce and become syrupy, then sprinkle a little salt over the steaks and serve immediately with the reduced wine spooned over.

Steak and Kidney Hotpot

For four people:

1½ lb chuck steak, trimmed and cut into 1-inch cubes	½ pint beef stock (made from a cube)
½ lb ox kidney, trimmed and cut fairly small	3 or 4 drops Worcestershire sauce
1½ lb potatoes	Beef dripping
2 medium onions, roughly chopped	Melted butter
1 rounded tablespoon flour	Salt and freshly milled black pepper

Pre-heat the oven to gas mark 2 (300°F).

First, melt some beef dripping in a large, wide-based saucepan and fry the onion in it to soften for about 10 minutes or so, then turn the heat up, add the cubes of beef and kidney and brown it all thoroughly, stirring and turning the meat as it browns.

Now sprinkle in a rounded tablespoon flour and stir it around to soak up the meat juices. Season well, add a few drops Worcestershire sauce, then gradually stir in the stock and bring to simmering point.

Now pour the meat mixture into a casserole or a pie dish, and cover it with the peeled potatoes cut into ½-inch slices and arranged in layers all over the meat. Season the potatoes, brush them with melted butter, then cover the casserole with a lid or foil and bake in the oven for 2½ to 3 hours.

During the last 40 minutes of the cooking time, remove the foil or lid so the potatoes can get brown and crisp.

Steak, Kidney and Mushroom Pie

To serve four people:

for the filling:

1½ lb chuck steak, cut into
  1-inch cubes
6 oz ox kidney, chopped
¼ lb dark-gilled mushrooms
2 medium onions
1 tablespoon beef dripping
1½ tablespoons flour

¾ pint beef stock (made with a
  cube)
½ teaspoon Worcestershire
  sauce
½ teaspoon dried mixed herbs
Salt and freshly milled black
  pepper

Start by frying the onions in the dripping, in a large saucepan, for a few minutes. Then add the steak and the kidney and brown nicely, stirring now and then. Next add the flour and have another good stir.

Season with freshly milled black pepper and salt, add the herbs and Worcestershire sauce, then gradually stir in the stock. Add the sliced mushrooms, bring to simmering point and simmer gently for about 2 hours, or until the meat is tender. When cooked, taste to check the seasoning and pour it all into an oval pie dish.

Pre-heat the oven to gas mark 7 (425°F). Make a suet crust pastry with:

12 oz self-raising flour
6 oz shredded beef suet

Cold water
A pinch of pepper and salt

Mix the pastry to a smooth elastic dough, then roll it out on a lightly floured board until it is about 1 inch larger all round than the pie dish. Now cut a 1-inch strip all round, dampen the edge of the pie dish and press the pastry strip on, then dampen the strip and lay the rest of the pastry on top, pressing it down to form a seal around the edge. Flute the edge and make a small ventilation hole in the centre. Bake the pie for 30 to 40 minutes, until the pastry is golden-brown.

Steak and Kidney Pudding

Quantities for four people:

1 lb chuck steak
½ lb ox kidney
1 medium onion, sliced
2 level tablespoons well-
 seasoned flour
Water and Worcestershire
 sauce

for the pastry:
12 oz self-raising flour
6 oz shredded suet
Pepper, salt and cold water

Just mix the suet with the flour, add seasoning and enough cold
water to make a fairly elastic dough that leaves the bowl cleanly.
Keep a quarter of the pastry for a lid, roll out the rest and line a
well-buttered 2 pint pudding basin with it. Now, chop the steak
and kidney into smallish pieces, toss them all in seasoned flour
and pack them into the lined basin – tucking in a few slices of
onion here and there. Now add enough cold water to reach almost
to the top of the meat, then a few drops of Worcestershire sauce.

Roll out the pastry lid, dampen the edges and put it on the
pudding, sealing thoroughly. Now cover with a double sheet of
foil (with a pleat in the centre to allow for expansion), tie with
string and place it in a steamer over boiling water, and steam for
4½ hours. You may find you need to add more boiling water
half-way through.

Beef Stew with Parsley Dumplings

For four to six people:

2 lb good stewing beef, cubed
1 tablespoon beef dripping
2 large carrots, sliced
2 large onions, sliced
1½ oz well seasoned flour
½ pint stock
1 teaspoon Worcestershire
 sauce
1 bay leaf
½ teaspoon thyme
Salt and freshly milled black
 pepper

for the dumplings:
4 oz self-raising flour
2 oz shredded suet
1 level tablespoon fresh
 chopped parsley
Salt and pepper

The best utensil for this is a flameproof casserole to use on top of the stove, or a large heavy saucepan. First melt the dripping and toss the cubes of meat in seasoned flour. When the dripping is fairly hot and sizzling, add the meat and brown it all over quickly, turning it from time to time.

Then add the onions and carrots and, keeping the heat high, brown those a little too, stirring them down to the base of the pan. Now pour in the stock, the Worcestershire sauce, thyme and bay leaf, season and put a lid on, then let it simmer very gently on top of the stove for about 2½ hours, or until the meat is tender.

To make the dumplings, mix the flour, suet and parsley together, season with salt and pepper, and mix to a smooth elastic dough with cold water. Divide the mixture and roll up in to six dumplings, turn the heat up a bit under the casserole or saucepan, add the dumplings and simmer them with a lid on for 20 minutes at the end of the cooking time. Serve immediately.

Poor Man's Stroganoff

Quantities for four people:

2 lb chuck steak
2 medium onions, sliced
10½-oz tin condensed
    mushroom soup
2 oz plain flour
5-oz carton natural yoghurt

1 level dessertspoon tomato
    purée
2 oz butter
Grated nutmeg
Salt and freshly milled black
    pepper

First, cut the meat into thinnish strips (about 1½ inches long), then melt the butter in a flameproof casserole and gently cook the sliced onions in it for about 5 minutes. Now add the meat and cook that for about 5 minutes also (stirring it around to colour it on all sides).

Now sprinkle in the flour, stir it again to soak up the juices, then stir in the tomato purée, followed by the contents of the tin of condensed soup and, finally, the yoghurt. Have another really good stir, add a little salt and freshly milled black pepper and a scraping of nutmeg, put on the lid and let it simmer gently for 1½ to 2 hours, or until the meat is tender. Taste to check the seasoning, and serve with rice.

Ossobuco

For four people:

4 large pieces shin of veal (approximately 2 inches thick)
½ pint dry white wine
¾ lb tomatoes, peeled, seeded and chopped
1 large clove garlic, finely chopped

Grated rind of a small lemon
2 heaped tablespoons fresh chopped parsley
Butter
Salt and freshly milled black pepper

In a wide shallow flameproof casserole melt the butter and fry the pieces of veal to brown them lightly on both sides. Keep them arranged upright in the pan, then pour the wine over, let it bubble and reduce a bit, adding the tomatoes and some freshly milled black pepper and salt. Put a lid on the casserole and let it cook gently on top of the stove for about 1 hour, then take the lid off and let it cook for another 30 minutes or so, or until the meat is tender and the sauce reduced. Before serving, mix the garlic. parsley and lemon rind together, then sprinkle it all over the meat,

Serve with rice, and don't forget to dig the marrow out from the centre of the bone – it is delicious.

Picnic Pie

For four people:

½ lb back rib of veal, trimmed and chopped small
½ lb chump end of pork, trimmed and chopped small (if you can't get veal, use all pork)
4 slices streaky bacon, diced
1 medium potato, peeled and chopped
1 small clove garlic, crushed
¼ teaspoon dried thyme

¼ level teaspoon powdered allspice
1 tablespoon stock (or water)
2 level tablespoons fresh chopped parsley
Salt and freshly milled black pepper

6 oz shortcrust pastry
1 beaten egg

For this recipe you need a greased 7-inch enamel pie plate. Preheat the oven to gas mark 6 (400°F).

First, place the chopped meats and bacon in a mixing bowl and add all the other ingredients (except the pastry and beaten egg). Now, mix them all thoroughly together, with a good seasoning of salt and pepper.

Divide the pastry into halves and roll out one half, and line the pie plate with it. Pile the meat mixture evenly on the pastry, dampen the edges, then roll out the other pastry half and fit it over to form a lid, sealing well all round, trimming and pinching (or fluting) the edges. Make a small hole in the centre of the lid, and if you have time you can use the trimmings to make a few leaves etc. for decoration.

Now brush the pie with beaten egg, place it in the oven, then after 10 minutes reduce the heat to gas mark 4 (350°F) and bake for a further 15 minutes. If the pastry gets a bit too brown during cooking, cover it with foil. Allow the pie to cool, then wrap it (plate as well) in a double thickness of foil ready to take on the picnic.

Kettner's Oxford Sausages

For two or three people:

½ lb minced veal
½ lb minced pork (an obliging butcher will provide you with these)
2 oz shredded beef suet
½ small onion, grated
2 thick slices bread from a large loaf (crusts removed)
1½ tablespoons milk
1 teaspoon grated lemon peel

3 fresh sage leaves, chopped small (or ¼ teaspoon dried)
¼ whole nutmeg, freshly grated
¼ teaspoon chopped thyme (fresh or dried)
1½ tablespoons seasoned flour
Lard
Salt, freshly milled black pepper

Take a large bowl and mix both meats and the suet together very thoroughly, then mix in the grated onion. Soak the bread in milk, squeeze the excess liquid out, and mix that in too, also very thoroughly. Now add the lemon peel, sage, nutmeg and thyme, and a good seasoning of salt and freshly milled black pepper. Again the mixing is very important and should not be skimped.

Next, take about a tablespoon of the mixture, press it together then roll into a sausage shape on a clean surface. Roll it in seasoned flour – and carry on like that until all your sausages are made.

Fry them in hot lard to brown all round, then reduce the heat to medium to cook them through. They take about 15 to 20 minutes in all. Drain them on crumpled kitchen paper and serve with sauté potatoes, a crisp salad and Oxford sauce.

Oxford Sauce
This recipe comes from one of the greatest English cookery writers, Eliza Acton, in her *Modern Cookery for Private Families* (1845).

The ingredients are:

1 tablespoon dark soft brown sugar

1 heaped teaspoon made-up English mustard

1 level teaspoon salt

A good seasoning of freshly milled black pepper

1 tablespoon wine vinegar

4 tablespoons mild olive oil

Place the mustard, brown sugar, vinegar and seasonings in a screw-top jar and leave them to stand for about an hour (for the sugar and salt to dissolve). Then add the oil, replace the lid and shake as vigorously as you can to amalgamate everything. Shake once more, just before serving.

Veal with Tarragon

For four people:

1½ lb boned shoulder of veal, cut into smallish cubes

1 bunch spring carrots, scraped and cut into 1-inch pieces

2 onions, roughly chopped

3 oz butter

1 rounded tablespoon flour

½ pint chicken stock

¼ pint dry white wine

¼ pint soured cream

1½ tablespoons fresh chopped tarragon (or 1 dessertspoon dried)

Salt and freshly milled black pepper

Pre-heat the oven to gas mark 3 (325°F).

Heat the butter gently in a large flameproof casserole and let the onion gently cook in it for about 6 minutes, then add the veal, turn the heat up a little and just colour the veal lightly on all sides, stirring it round. Add the tarragon, then stir in the flour and add the white wine and stock bit by bit, stirring well after each addition. Add the carrots, season with salt and freshly milled pepper, then put a lid on the casserole and let it cook in the oven for 1½ to 2 hours, or until the veal is tender. Ten minutes before the end of the cooking stir in the soured cream, replace the lid and allow it to heat.

Serve with rice and a crisp green side salad.

Cassoulet

To serve six:

¾ lb white haricot beans
½ boned shoulder lamb (ask the butcher to take the bone out for you), the inside half not the leg half
1 lb belly of pork, boned and cut into strips
½ lb streaky bacon (in one piece)
¼ lb garlic sausage (in one piece)

4 juniper berries
2 medium onions, chopped
1 bay leaf
2 cloves garlic
1 sprig thyme
1 small sprig rosemary
A few parsley stalks
5 oz fresh white breadcrumbs
Salt and freshly milled black pepper

There is no need to soak the beans overnight – just wash them thoroughly in a couple of changes of water then place them in a saucepan with about 3 pints cold water, bring them up to simmering point and let them simmer for about 2 minutes. Then take them off the heat and let them soak for 1 hour.

Meanwhile, you can prepare the other ingredients. First trim the lamb of any really excess fat and cut it into very large chunks. Using your sharpest knife, pare the rind from the bacon as thinly as possible and chop it into small pieces. Then do exactly the same with the pork rinds.

Leave the pork slices whole but chop the bacon into six chunks, and then peel and chop the garlic sausage into largish chunks. Next tie the thyme, rosemary, parsley stalks and bay leaf together with string in a little bunch. Then finally peel and crush the garlic cloves and crush the juniper berries with the back of a tablespoon.

When the beans have finished soaking, drain them in a colander and discard the water. Then put the beans in a saucepan, together with the bacon (plus the chopped pork and bacon rinds), garlic sausage, onions, garlic, juniper berries and the bunch of herbs. Season with pepper, but no salt as the bacon will be salty.

Now pour over about 2½ pints cold water, or enough to cover, and heat to simmering point; simmer gently for 1½ hours. Halfway through this cooking time, having pre-heated the oven to gas mark 3 (325°F), place the lamb and pork in a roasting tin and cook them in the oven for 45 minutes.

At the end of this time the beans etc. will be ready. Place a large sieve or colander over a bowl and drain the contents of the saucepan; remove the herbs and reserve the liquid. Butter a 5-pint earthenware casserole, arrange half the bean mixture over the base, then arrange the pieces of pork and lamb on top. Season with salt and freshly milled black pepper, then cover with the rest of the bean mixture.

Measure ¾ pint of the reserved liquid, pour it into the casserole, then cover the surface completely with breadcrumbs. Place the casserole uncovered in the oven and let it continue cooking for 1½ hours.

Collared Breast of Lamb

Ask your butcher to remove all the bones etc. from a nice large breast of lamb. The rest of the ingredients for two people are:

2 oz fresh breadcrumbs
Grated rind of ½ lemon
¼ whole nutmeg, grated
1 tablespoon freshly chopped mint
1 tablespoon freshly chopped parsley

1 medium onion, very finely chopped
1 teaspoon finely crushed rosemary
1 small egg, beaten
Salt and freshly milled black pepper

Pre-heat the oven to gas mark 4 (350°F).

In a mixing bowl mix the breadcrumbs and onion, parsley, mint and rosemary, then add the nutmeg and lemon rind. Mix well, adding a good seasoning of pepper and salt. Stir in the beaten egg to bind the stuffing together, then spread it evenly over the breast of lamb and roll it up gently and not too tightly. Tuck the flap end over, then tie the meat in three places with string – again not too tightly. Press back any bits of stuffing that fall out, then wrap the meat in foil, place it on a roasting tin and bake for 1½ hours.

Unwrap the foil, baste with the juices and brown for a further ½ hour. Serve the meat cut in thick slices with thin gravy made with the juices, and some redcurrant jelly.

Lamb Chops Baked with Herbs and Breadcrumbs

The ingredients for four are:

4 large chump chops
6 level tablespoons fresh chopped parsley
6 level tablespoons softened butter
4 oz fresh white breadcrumbs

Grated rind and juice of ½ lemon
2 cloves garlic, crushed
Salt and freshly milled black pepper

Pre-heat the oven to gas mark 4 (350°F).

First dry the lamb chops on some kitchen paper, then in a large bowl mix the breadcrumbs with the softened butter. Add the parsley, the rind and juice of half a lemon and the 2 crushed cloves of garlic, then season well with salt and freshly milled black pepper; using a large fork mix very thoroughly until all the ingredients are evenly combined. Now coat each chop all over with an equal quantity of the mixture. Arrange the chops in a baking tin and bake for about 45 to 50 minutes.

Serve with buttered new potatoes and a green side salad. If you want to, and have the time, you can prepare these chops well in advance, which will give all the flavours a chance to penetrate a bit more.

Marinaded Lamb Chops

For two people:

4 loin chops
4 tablespoons dry white wine
4 tablespoons olive oil
2 cloves garlic, cut in slivers
1 small bay leaf, crumpled

1 teaspoon oregano
1 tablespoon lemon juice
Salt and freshly milled black pepper

First, mix all the marinade ingredients together, place the lamb chops in a shallow dish and pour the mixture over them, adding a seasoning of salt and freshly milled pepper. Leave them to marinade for 3 or 4 hours, turning them over now and then. When the time is up, pre-heat the grill at full blast for 10 minutes and grill the chops for about 6 minutes on each side (according to how you like them), basting with a little of the marinade mixture.

Serve with Onion Rice (see p. 153).

Mustard Glazed Lamb Chops

For two people:

4 medium lamb chops
4 level teaspoons mixed mustard (English or French, as you like)

4 heaped teaspoons demerara sugar
Salt and freshly milled black pepper

Before you start, turn the grill on to get nice and hot, then wipe the chops and dry them with some kitchen paper. Season with pepper and salt, spread each chop with mustard on both sides, then dip each side in the demerara sugar. Brown them quickly on both sides under the hot grill, now reduce the heat to prevent the chops burning and cook for about 20 to 30 minutes, depending on their thickness.

Serve with Onion Rice (see p. 153).

Leftover Lamb Curry

For two or three people:

1 lb (approx.) cooked lamb, cut into bite-sized pieces
¾ lb tomatoes, peeled and chopped
1 medium onion, chopped small
1 dessert apple, peeled and chopped
1 level dessertspoon flour
2 rounded teaspoons Madras curry powder (or according to taste)

1 clove garlic, crushed
4–5 tablespoons hot water
1 heaped teapoon mango chutney
Salt and freshly milled black pepper
Lamb dripping or butter

In a thick-based saucepan, melt the fat and gently cook the onion and garlic for about 8 minutes, then stir in the pieces of apple. Let them cook for a minute or two, and next add the lamb. When that has cooked for a couple of minutes sprinkle in the curry

93

powder and the flour, stir around and let that cook for a couple of minutes. Finally stir in the tomatoes and chutney and 4 tablespoons hot water, bring to simmering point (still stirring), season with salt and pepper, put a lid on and simmer gently for about 25 minutes. Taste half-way through to see if it needs more curry powder, and add a drop more water if it looks too thick. Serve with boiled rice and mango chutney.

Baked Lamb with Butter and Herbs

Quantities for four:

1 shoulder English lamb (about 4 lb)	2 tablespoons approx. fresh chopped mint
1½ oz butter, softened	¼ pint dry white wine
1 teaspoon crushed rosemary (dried)	Salt and freshly milled black pepper
1 clove garlic	

Pre-heat the oven to gas mark 5 (375°F).

First of all, crush the rosemary on a chopping board by pressing it firmly with the back of a tablespoon, and mix it with the butter, together with the chopped mint, ½ teaspoon salt and a few screws of black pepper.

Crush the garlic with the tip of a kitchen knife or in a garlic press and add it to the butter mixture.

Now, mash with a fork to mix everything evenly, make a few stabs in the joint with a skewer (so that the flavour of the herbs can get in) and spread the butter mixture all over. Put a double sheet of cooking foil into a roasting tin, place the joint on top, wrap it up and seal it well.

Then into the oven with it for 2½ hours, or rather less if you like your lamb pink. Either way, during the last 20 minutes or so, open up the foil to let the meat brown a little, When it is cooked, remove the joint to a warm place, empty all the juices into the roasting tin. Tip them into the corner and spoon off all the fat.

To the remaining juices add the white wine and let it bubble over the heat to reduce slightly. Carve the lamb and serve with the sauce poured over. Roast potatoes and a green salad would be fine with this.

94

Baked Lamb with Coriander

For two or three people:

½ shoulder lamb	1 tablespoon coriander seeds,
2 cloves garlic	crushed
	Dripping

In winter when fresh herbs are unavailable coriander seed makes a delicious and equally good alternative. Pre-heat the oven to gas mark 5 (375°F).

Place the meat in a roasting tin and, using a small sharp knife, make 6 to 8 evenly placed incisions. Into these slits push slivers of garlic and about 1 tablespoon coriander seeds (crushed a bit first, using either a pestle and mortar or the back of a tablespoon). If you are cooking a whole shoulder or a leg of lamb double these quantities. The amount of garlic is up to you; I suggest either 1 large clove or 2 small ones.

Add a knob of dripping to the roasting tin and cook for 30 minutes to the pound. When the lamb is cooked, carve it in thick slices, strain off the fat from the roasting tin and add a little wine to the juice to make a gravy. Redcurrant jelly is a nice accompaniment.

Greek Lamb on the Bone

For four people:

1 small leg of lamb, cut into four thick slices and left on the bone	2 aubergines, cubed
	4 large tomatoes, peeled and sliced
4 cloves garlic, peeled	2 tablespoons olive oil
1 level teaspoon dried oregano	Salt and freshly milled black pepper
2 large onions, thinly sliced	

Pre-heat the oven to gas mark 2 (300°F).

Dry the meat with some kitchen paper, then make a little slit somewhere near the bone in each slice and insert a peeled clove of garlic. Rub the lamb pieces all over with about one tablespoon of olive oil, then pour another tablespoon of oil into a meat roasting tin. Arrange the meat in the tin, sprinkle on the oregano and a seasoning of salt and pepper, then roast slowly (uncovered) for $1\frac{1}{2}$ hours.

When the time is up, take it out of the oven then tilt the roasting tin and spoon off most of the fat. Place the tin over a medium heat on top of the stove, then stir in the vegetables and let them soften a bit, stirring them well into the meat juices and seasoning them with salt and pepper. Now put everything back into the oven for a further $1\frac{1}{2}$ hours, or until the meat and vegetables are tender. A crisp green salad with a sharp lemon dressing would be a nice accompaniment.

Lancashire Hotpot

This is the traditional Lancashire recipe. Quantities to serve four:

1 lb neck of mutton or lamb with the excess fat removed (this should be best-end cutlets, though middle and scrag-end mixed will also do)
1 sheep's kidney, sliced (to flavour the gravy)
1 lb onions, peeled and sliced
2 lb potatoes

$\frac{1}{2}$ pint hot water
Worcestershire sauce
Dripping
2 tablespoons well-seasoned flour
1 bay leaf
Salt, freshly milled black pepper

Pre-heat the oven to gas mark 3 ($325°$ F).

First, grease the inside of a ovenproof casserole or cooking pot with dripping, add a bay leaf and heat it through in the oven for 10 minutes. In the meantime, you can be preparing the onions and potatoes, which should both be peeled and sliced, the onions into thin rounds, and the potatoes in thick slices.

Wipe the lamb cutlets and kidney and coat them lightly with seasoned flour. Now, take your 'hot pot' from the oven and put in it first a layer of potatoes, then the meat followed by the sliced onions, and finish off with a layer of potatoes arranged all over the top like slates on a roof. While you are packing the pot, remember to season each layer with salt and freshly milled pepper.

Now measure $\frac{1}{2}$ pint hot water, add a few drops of Worcestershire sauce to it and pour it over everything. Then scatter a few flecks of dripping over the potatoes, put on the lid and return the pot to the oven for $1\frac{1}{2}$ hours.

At that point remove the lid and let it cook for a further 40 minutes, allowing the potatoes to brown nicely (if they do not seem to be browning, turn the heat up a bit). The hotpot should be served straight from the pot on to warmed plates with a spare plate on the table for the bones.

Moussaka

Quantities for four:

1 lb minced lamb (or beef)
$\frac{1}{2}$ lb onions, peeled and sliced
2 cloves garlic, chopped
3 medium aubergines, cut into $\frac{1}{2}$-inch rounds
2 tablespoons tomato purée
3 fl. oz red or white wine
1 teaspoon ground cinnamon
1 tablespoon fresh chopped parsley
Salt, pepper and plenty of cooking oil

for the topping:
3 oz butter
3 oz plain flour
2 oz grated Cheddar cheese
1 pint milk
2 eggs
Freshly grated nutmeg
Salt and freshly milled black pepper

Start by putting the sliced aubergines into a colander, sprinkling them with salt, then placing a plate with a heavy weight on it on top of them. Leave them like that for 30 minutes, so that some of the excess moisture will drain off.

Now, gently fry the onions and garlic in olive oil for 5 minutes or so, then add the minced meat and brown it, stirring all the time with a wooden spoon to break down the lumps.

When it has browned, in a small basin, mix the tomato purée, wine, parsley and cinnamon with a good seasoning of salt and pepper, then pour this mixture over the meat and onions. Stir it in, then with the heat turned low you can leave it to simmer gently while you get on with the aubergines.

Heat some olive oil in a frying pan. Dry the aubergines in a clean cloth, and fry each slice both sides to a golden-brown colour, then arrange the slices on some kitchen paper to drain. You will need plenty of oil for this operation, as aubergines soak it up very quickly.

When the aubergines are ready, arrange some of the slices in the bottom of a casserole then spread some of the meat mixture over them. Then more aubergines – and so on until everything is used up.

Now to make the topping, melt the butter in a saucepan, stir in the flour and add the milk, bit by bit, stirring vigorously all the time till you have a thick smooth white sauce. Stir in the grated cheese and season with salt and pepper and lots of freshly grated nutmeg. Allow the sauce to cool, then whisk two eggs, first thoroughly on their own, then into the sauce.

Pour the sauce over the meat and aubergines and bake in the centre of the oven, pre-heated to gas mark 4 (350°F), for 1 hour, by which time the top will be golden and fluffy.

Mutton and Barley Stew

Ingredients for four people:

2½ lb lean middle neck and scrag-end mutton or lamb (with the excess fat removed)	1 large potato, peeled and sliced
¾ lb onions, sliced	1 tablespoon pearl barley
½ lb carrots, sliced	2 tablespoons seasoned flour
2 medium leeks, washed and sliced	Hot water
	Salt and freshly ground black pepper

Start by wiping the pieces of meat and coating them in seasoned flour. Then arrange them in the bottom of a saucepan. Now over the meat arrange some slices of onion, carrot, leek and potato. Season well with salt and pepper. Then put in some more meat – and so on, until everything is in. Finally sprinkle in the barley. Pour in about 2 pints hot water and bring it to simmering point. Spoon off any scum that rises, then put the lid on and let it all simmer very gently for about 2 hours.

About 15 minutes before the end of the cooking time make the dumplings. The ingredients for these are:

4 oz self-raising flour	1 tablespoon fresh chopped parsley
2 oz shredded suet	Pepper and salt

Sift the flour into a mixing bowl, add some pepper and a pinch of salt and all the parsley (if fresh parsley is not available – just make plain dumplings). Then add the suet and mix thoroughly, but don't rub it in.

Add enough cold water to make a fairly stiff but elastic dough that leaves the bowl cleanly, then divide it into eight and roll each portion into a dumpling shape.

When the stew is ready, using a draining spoon take out all the meat and vegetables and transfer them on to a large warm serving dish. Cover with a piece of foil and keep warm in the bottom of a very low oven.

Now bring the liquid to a very fast boil (better taste it first, though, to see if there is enough seasoning). Put the dumplings into the bubbling liquid, replace the lid and let them simmer, without coming off the boil, for 20 to 25 minutes.

Serve the meat and vegetables with the dumplings all round and some of the gravy poured over (and the rest in a sauce boat).

Navarin of Lamb

For four people:

2½ lb middle neck of lamb, cut into pieces	½ teaspoon mixed herbs
Salt and freshly milled black pepper	8 small onions, peeled and left whole
Dripping	6 small turnips, peeled and quartered
2 tablespoons flour	6 small thin carrots, cut into 1-inch lengths
1¼ pints hot water	
1 level tablespoon tomato purée	12 small new potatoes, scraped
1 clove garlic, crushed	1 level teaspoon brown sugar

Heat some dripping in a large flameproof casserole, season the meat with salt and freshly milled black pepper, then fry in the hot fat till brown on all sides. Now sprinkle in the flour and cook gently, stirring to soak up the juices. Next, add the water, tomato purée, crushed garlic and mixed herbs, bring slowly to the boil, stirring everything round a bit, then put a lid on and simmer very gently for 45 minutes. Meanwhile, fry the prepared onions, turnips and carrots and when the 45 minutes is up add them to the casserole, with the potatoes, bring to simmering point again, add the sugar, cover and simmer very gently for a further 45 minutes.

Stuffed Peppers

For four people:

4 medium-sized peppers (green or red)	2 level tablespoons currants
¾ lb (approx.) cooked lamb, cut in very small pieces	2 dessertspoons pine nuts (healthfood shops sell them)
2 medium onions, peeled and sliced	½ teaspoon ground cinnamon
2 cloves garlic, chopped small	½ teaspoon marjoram
14-oz tin Italian tomatoes	1 large teacup long-grain rice
4 teaspoons tomato purée	2½ teacups boiling water
	Salt, pepper, dripping

Pre-heat the oven to gas mark 5 (375°F).

First, prepare the rice by melting some lamb dripping in a saucepan, then stir in the rice and when it has soaked up all the fat pour in 2½ cups boiling water. Add salt, stir once, then cover the saucepan, and simmer until all the liquid has been absorbed (20 to 25 minutes).

Meanwhile, in a little more dripping, fry the sliced onions and garlic for a minute or two, then add the meat, currants and pine nuts. Season very well with salt and freshly milled black pepper, then stir in the cinnamon and marjoram, and two of the tomatoes plus a tablespoon of juice from the contents of the tin. Now turn the heat very low and leave it all to simmer gently while you prepare the peppers.

Slice the stalk ends off the peppers, remove the core and the seeds, and run each one under the cold tap (to make sure all the seeds are out). Then sit them upright in a smallish casserole – so there is not too much room for them to topple over.

By this time your rice should be ready, so tip it out into the frying pan with the other ingredients and stir well to blend it all in.

It is probably a good idea to have a taste just now, to make sure you have enough pepper and salt. Spoon the mixture into the peppers, packing it down to get as much in as possible, the remaining rice mixture can be placed all round the base of the peppers – and this will help to keep them sitting up.

Finally, put 1 teaspoon tomato purée on top of each one, then pour the rest of the tomatoes all over. Put a lid on the casserole, and cook for 40 to 45 minutes, or until the peppers feel tender when tested with a skewer.

Ragout of Mutton

For two people:

2 lb neck of lamb (this can be middle and scrag-end)
2 tablespoons dripping (preferably lamb)
2 medium onions, roughly chopped
1 or 2 cloves garlic, crushed
1 sprig fresh thyme (or $\frac{1}{2}$ teaspoon dried)

1 bay leaf
1 heaped tablespoon flour
1 pint boiling water
$\frac{3}{4}$ lb small new potatoes
4 medium tomatoes, peeled
Salt and pepper

Pre-heat the oven to gas mark 2 (300° F).

Trim any excess fat off the meat, season it with salt and freshly milled black pepper, and brown the meat in the dripping, a few pieces at a time. When they are all nicely brown, transfer them to a casserole using a draining spoon. Now gently fry the onions and crushed garlic for 10 minutes or so to soften, and transfer these to the casserole with the meat, throwing in a bay leaf and a sprig of thyme.

Next, over a low heat stir the flour into the juices left in the pan, and then gradually add 1 pint boiling water from the kettle, stirring after each addition. When all the water is in, bring to simmering point, season and pour it over the meat, etc. in the casserole. Put the lid on the casserole and bake for 1 hour.

Then add the peeled potatoes and the whole peeled tomatoes, taste to check the seasoning (add a bit more if necessary), put the lid on and leave for a further hour, or until the potatoes are tender.

PORK AND BACON

Pork Braised with Apples and Cider

To serve four:

4 thick belly pork slices or
4 pork chops
6 rashers unsmoked streaky
bacon
1 large cooking apple, peeled,
cored and sliced
2 medium onions, chopped
small
¼ pint dry cider

2 garlic cloves, finely chopped
6 juniper berries, crushed with
the back of a spoon
1½ lb potatoes, peeled and
thickly sliced
Lard, and a little butter
Salt and freshly milled black
pepper

Pre-heat the oven to gas mark 2 (300°F).

Fry the pork slices in hot lard to colour them on both sides, then
arrange them in a wide shallow casserole. Now fry the bacon
slices a little, until the fat starts to run, and using a draining
spoon transfer them to the casserole on top of the pork. Season
with pepper and just a little salt (there is some already in the
bacon) and sprinkle over the crushed juniper berries and chopped
garlic.

Then, arrange the slices of apple and the chopped onions all
over. Pour in the cider, and finish off by arranging the potatoes
on top, overlapping each other. Season the potatoes with a little
salt and pepper, and place a few flecks of butter here and there.
Now cover the casserole with a sheet of greaseproof paper or foil,
put on a close-fitting lid, and let it cook slowly in the oven for
3 hours.

During the last 45 minutes of the cooking time, take the lid and
the paper off so that the potatoes can brown nicely. This dish
goes particularly well with braised red cabbage (see p. 144).

(Note: You may need to turn the heat up to very high during
the last 10 minutes of cooking to brown the potatoes sufficiently.)

Pork Chops with Cream and Mushrooms

Quantities for four people:

4 large pork chops	1 heaped tablespoon plain flour
½ lb mushrooms	Dried thyme
¼ pint double cream	Butter
Juice of a medium-sized lemon	Salt and pepper

Pre-heat the oven to gas mark 4 (350°F).

Place a large double sheet of cooking foil on a meat roasting tin (it must be large enough to wrap the chops in). In a frying pan brown the chops nicely on both sides in butter, then transfer them on to the foil, season with salt and freshly milled black pepper and sprinkle each one with a little dried thyme.

Now chop the mushrooms roughly and fry them in the same pan that the meat was browned in, adding a little more butter if necessary. Next add the lemon juice, let that bubble a minute and then throw in the flour. Stir with a wooden spoon until you have a rather soggy-looking lump of mushroom mixture (it is supposed to be like that). Spoon the mixture over the pork chops, a little on each, then pour the double cream over. Wrap up the foil, sealing it securely, and bake for 1 hour.

Serve the chops with the delicious juice poured over and, since this is very rich, keep the accompanying vegetables simple.

(Note: When cooked, the cream takes on a slightly curdled appearance – this does not in any way spoil the delicious flavour.)

Pork Chops with Sage and Apples

To serve four people:

4 lean pork chops	1 medium onion, peeled and sliced into rings
4 tablespoons dried wholemeal breadcrumbs (from health-food shops)	1 large cooking apple, peeled and sliced into rings
3 level dessertspoons dried crumbled sage	Butter, oil
1 small egg	Salt and freshly milled black pepper

First, mix the sage and breadcrumbs together and season well with pepper and salt. Beat up the egg, and dip the pork chops first in the egg, then in the breadcrumbs and sage, pressing firmly all round so that they get a good even coating.

Now heat up some oil and butter together in a frying pan, brown the chops quickly on both sides with the fat fairly hot, then lower the heat and let them gently cook through (which will take 25 to 30 minutes depending on the thickness of the chops).

While that is happening, in another frying pan melt a little more butter and oil and fry the apple and onion rings. Drain everything on crumpled greaseproof paper before serving. Baked jacket potatoes with plenty of butter, cream and chives go well with this.

Stuffed Pork Chops

Quantities for three people:

3 thick pork loin chops

for the stuffing:

1 tablespoon butter	5 tablespoons chopped parsley
1 tablespoon oil	1 teaspoon lemon juice
1 onion, chopped very small	1 level teaspoon fennel seeds, crushed
1 clove garlic, crushed	
1 oz rye bread, diced	1 tablespoon double cream
5 tablespoons chopped celery leaves	Salt and freshly milled black pepper

to cook:

2 tablespoons butter	¼ pint dry white wine
Flour	

Pre-heat the oven to gas mark 4 (350°F).

Heat the butter and oil and fry the chopped onion and crushed garlic until the onion is soft. Remove the pan from the heat, then stir in the diced rye bread and the rest of the stuffing ingredients. Now cut a sort of pocket in each chop, and fill each with some of the stuffing mixture, pressing it in well, then heat the butter in a casserole. Dip the chops on each side in some flour, then brown them in the hot fat.

Drain off the excess fat from the casserole, then, arranging the chops side by side, pour the wine over them. Cover with a lid and bake in the oven for 30 minutes, then remove the lid and bake for a further 30 minutes. Skim any fat from the juices remaining in the casserole and serve the chops with the juices poured over.

Pork with Coriander

For a quick meal for two people:

1 lb pork fillet
1 level tablespoon lard (or oil)
¼ pint dry white wine
¾ teaspoon ground cumin seed
1 level teaspoon ground
  coriander seed

1 clove garlic, crushed
4 thin slices lemon, cut into
  quarters
1 level teaspoon brown sugar
Salt and freshly milled black
  pepper

Cut the meat into 1-inch cubes, removing the excess fat where necessary. Heat the lard or oil in a large saucepan, then fry the pork briskly in the hot fat until golden-brown on all sides.

Now turn the heat down, and add the wine, cumin, coriander and garlic, and season with a little salt and freshly milled black pepper. Stir everything together, bring to simmering point, then cover and simmer very gently for 20 to 25 minutes, or until the pork is tender.

Now take off the lid, add the lemon slices and sugar, and cook (uncovered) until the sauce is a little reduced and thickened slightly. Serve immediately, with Onion Rice (see p. 153) and maybe a side salad.

Pork Fillet with Dates and Walnuts

To serve two people:

1 pork fillet (approx. 1 lb)
2 heaped tablespoons finely
  chopped walnuts
1 small glass (5 fl. oz) port
8 fl. oz chicken or veal stock
1 dessertspoon plain flour

Butter
Salt and freshly milled black
  pepper
2 heaped tablespoons finely
  chopped dates
2 sprigs watercress

First, prepare the fillet by trimming it and, using a sharp knife, make a slit down the centre (to about 1 in. from each end). Now spread the fillet out so that the slit forms a sort of pocket.

Season the meat, then heat some butter (a large tablespoonful) in a largish pan, and sauté the fillet to a nice golden-brown colour all over – it needs to be about two-thirds cooked (for about 10 minutes), but avoid having the heat too high as the fillet must not go too hard and crusty on the outside.

Remove the meat and keep it warm, then add the dates and walnuts to the pan juices, adding a bit more butter if necessary. Cook the nuts and dates for a few minutes, then use three-quarters of them to stuff the pocket of the fillet.

Now sprinkle about 1 dessertspoon flour over the pan juices and the remaining nuts and dates (adding a little more butter if it needs it). Cook the flour for a minute or two to brown it, then with the heat turned up very high pour in the port, set it alight and rotate the pan till the flames die down (if you cook with electricity, heat the port in a small saucepan, set light to it and pour it flaming into the pan). Then add the stock, let the sauce bubble and reduce by about a third until it has a good consistency.

Taste to check the seasoning, then return the stuffed fillet to the pan and finish cooking it in the sauce. Serve it with the sauce poured over and garnished with watercress.

Pork with Prunes

To serve four people:

8 small noisettes pork (boned loin chops about 1-inch thick
1 dozen large prunes, soaked overnight in ¼ pint dry white wine
Seasoned flour

2 oz butter
¼ pint double cream
½ teaspoon redcurrant jelly
Salt and freshly milled black pepper

Place the soaked prunes and the wine together in a saucepan, and simmer gently for 30 minutes. Meanwhile, coat the noisettes in seasoned flour and fry them gently in butter, on both sides, till cooked through (15 to 20 minutes).

Now transfer them to a warmed serving dish, drain the prunes (reserving the liquid) and arrange them round the pork and keep warm.

Next add the prune liquor to the juices in the pan, boil for a few minutes to reduce the liquid a bit, then stir in the cream and redcurrant jelly.

Heat through until the jelly has dissolved, taste, season with salt and freshly milled pepper, then pour over the pork and prunes and serve.

Pork and Cider Hotpot

Quantities for four people:

1½ lb lean pork, cut into cubes	4 fl. oz cider
1 large cooking apple, peeled, cored and sliced	Lard
	Caster sugar
½ lb onions, sliced	Butter
4 oz prunes, halved and stoned (no need to pre-soak)	Salt and freshly milled black pepper
1½ lb potatoes	Sage

Pre-heat the oven to gas mark 3 (325°F).

Fry the pork in a little lard to brown nicely, then arrange it in the bottom of a shallow (and fairly wide) fireproof casserole. Season with pepper and salt and about a teaspoon of sage (fresh or dried) sprinkled over.

Now, fry the onion a little and put it round the pork with a few pieces of prune tucked here and there. Next arrange the apple slices all over and give them a very slight dusting of caster sugar. Finally, arrange the potato slices on top, getting them to overlap each other.

Season with some more pepper and salt, dot with a few flecks of butter and pour in the cider. Cover and bake for 1½ hours. When this time is up, raise the heat to mark 8 (450°F), remove the lid and cook for a further 20 minutes or so – until the potatoes have turned golden brown.

Roast Pork with Honey and Ginger

Quantities for four:

1 piece loin pork, 2½ lb (ask the butcher to score the skin)
1 tablespoon ground ginger
2 tablespoons clear honey
14 whole cloves
Salt and freshly milled black pepper
A little white wine

About 2 or 3 hours before you start to cook stand the pork on a plate, stick the cloves in all over (and down into the scored skin), rub the honey in all over and down the sides as well, then sprinkle the dried ginger over and rub that in a bit. Leave in a cool place so that the pork has a chance to absorb all the flavours.

Pre-heat the oven to gas mark 6 (400°F), transfer the meat on to a roasting tin, sprinkle with salt and pepper, and roast at that temperature for 15 minutes (no need to add oil or fat). Then lower the heat to gas mark 5 (375°F) and cook for a further 1½ to 2 hours. The pork skin or crackling turns completely black during the cooking; this is due to the honey caramelizing, It is not burning, and is supposed to look like that.

When it is cooked, transfer it on to a serving dish, spoon off the fat and rinse the roasting tin with white wine over a low heat to form a gravy. Carve the meat into thick slices and serve with a little of the gravy – and do make sure everyone gets some delicious caramelized crackling.

Stuffed Cabbage Leaves

Quantities for four or five people:

1 head green cabbage
  (weighing 2 to 3 lb)

for the stuffing:
1 lb lean minced pork
1 tablespoon oil
1 tablespoon butter
1 onion, finely chopped
1 garlic clove, crushed
2 oz cooked rice
2 eggs, beaten
2 tablespoons paprika
½ teaspoon dried marjoram
Salt and freshly milled black
  pepper

for the sauce:
14-oz tin tomatoes
¼ pint chicken stock
2–3 tablespoons soured cream

First, bring a large saucepan of salted water to the boil and place the cabbage in the water, stalk end up. Bring back to the boil and simmer for about 8 minutes, then leave to cool. Working with the cabbage stalk end up, cut the large outer leaves from the main stalk and peel them off one by one. Drain the leaves on kitchen paper – you will need about 15 leaves altogether. Now heat the oil and butter together and fry the chopped onion and garlic gently until the onion is soft and golden.

Put the minced pork in a bowl, add the onion and garlic and mix thoroughly with the rest of the stuffing ingredients, seasoning well. Now make a V-shaped cut to remove the thickest part of the stalk from the base of each leaf, place about 1 tablespoon stuffing in the centre of each leaf, fold in the sides and roll the leaf up tightly. Pack the rolled leaves closely in a casserole and pour the contents of the tin of tomatoes and the stock over, cover and cook very gently over a low heat for 1 to 1½ hours. Drain the rolls well, and set aside to keep warm. Now boil the juices remaining in the casserole to reduce by a third. Turn down the heat, stir in the soured cream, taste and season and pour the sauce over the rolls.

Boiled Bacon with Leek Sauce

Quantities for six people:

1 bacon joint (middle cut gammon, forehock or slipper), about 3½ lb
1 onion, stuck with 4 cloves

1 bay leaf
8 peppercorns
A few parsley stalks, if available

Place the bacon joint in a large saucepan with enough cold water to cover. Bring it up to simmering point, then throw out the water, cover the bacon with fresh water, add all the other ingredients and when it comes to simmering point again, cover and let it cook for 20 minutes to the pound, plus 20 minutes over (a joint weighing 3¾ lb will take 1½ hours).

Leek Sauce

4 leeks, prepared, chopped and washed thoroughly
2 oz butter
2 oz flour
¼ pint milk
¼ pint cream
¼ pint bacon stock
Pepper and nutmeg

When the bacon is almost ready (about 15 minutes before the end) melt the butter and gently soften the chopped leeks in it for about 10 minutes over a low heat with the lid on. Then remove the lid, stir in the flour and cook for a couple of minutes.

Now gradually add the milk, stirring vigorously after each addition, followed by the bacon stock and lastly the cream. Bring the sauce to simmering point and simmer very gently for about 3 minutes.

Season the sauce with pepper and a little nutmeg to taste (and salt if it needs it, although there is probably enough in the bacon stock).

Serve the well-drained bacon cut in thick slices, with the sauce handed round separately.

Braised Bacon in Cider

For six to eight people:

3 lb bacon joint
1 small potato, peeled
1 small onion, stuck with a few cloves
1 bay leaf
6 black peppercorns
½ pint dry cider
Water

to finish off:
1 small swede, cut into chunks
1 medium onion, sliced
2 large carrots, sliced
3 sticks celery, cut into chunks
2 oz butter
Freshly milled black pepper

Place the bacon in a saucepan with the potato, which will take care of any saltiness – no need to pre-soak it. Add the onion, cloves, bay leaf and peppercorns, then pour in the cider and enough cold water to just cover the joint. Put a lid on and simmer the bacon for 45 minutes.

Towards the end of that time, pre-heat the oven to gas mark 4 (350°F), and fry the prepared vegetables in butter to colour them lightly. Then arrange them in the bottom of a casserole, season with pepper, and after the 45 minutes are up, remove the bacon from the cooking liquid, cut off the skin with a sharp knife and place the bacon on top of the vegetables.

Pour in enough of the cooking liquid to just cover the vegetables, put a lid on the casserole and place it in the oven for a further 45 minutes. Serve the bacon cut in thick slices with the vegetables and some of the cooking liquid spooned over, and have some mustard on the table to go with it.

Spiced Baked Gammon with Cumberland Sauce

To serve six people:

- 1 piece middle-cut rolled gammon (about 3½ lb)
- 1 onion, peeled and stuck with a few cloves
- 1 potato, peeled
- 1 bay leaf
- 1 pint dry cider
- 2 dozen cloves
- 2 tablespoons dark brown sugar
- 1 tablespoon made mustard

Put the gammon into a saucepan that it fits nicely, together with the bay leaf and potato and onion (cut them in half if there is not much room). Now pour in ¾ pint cider and enough water to cover, bring it to the boil and simmer gently for 1 hour. Lift the gammon out of the cooking liquid, and when it is cool enough to handle, take a sharp knife, cut off the string and remove the skin. Then, standing it up with the fat side uppermost, score the fat diagonally, first one way then the other, so that it stands out in a diamond-shaped pattern.

Insert a clove into each diamond, spread on the mustard, then press the brown sugar all over (it is probably easiest to do this with your hands). Place the joint in a roasting tin with ¼ pint dry cider in the bottom and put it into the oven, pre-heated to gas mark 6 (400°F). Bake it for 45 minutes, basting it now and then with the cider.

(Note: mild-cured gammon usually does not need soaking, and the potato added to the initial cooking water will extract any saltiness – but if you are in any doubt, you can soak the meat for about 12 hours, changing the water once or twice).

Cut the meat into thick slices and serve with Cumberland Sauce.

Cumberland Sauce

4 large tablespoons redcurrant jelly (read the labels carefully and go for a make that guarantees a high fruit content)	1 medium orange
	1 medium lemon
	1 heaped teaspoon dry mustard powder
4 tablespoons port	1 heaped teaspoon powdered ginger

First, thinly pare off the rinds of both the lemon and the orange (either with a very sharp paring knife or a potato peeler) then cut them into very small strips, about ½ inch in length and as thin as possible. Boil the rinds in water for 5 minutes or so to extract any bitterness, then drain well in a sieve.

Now, place the redcurrant jelly in a saucepan with the port, and melt them together over a low heat for about 5 or 10 minutes. The redcurrant jelly will not melt completely, so it is best to sieve it afterwards to get rid of any obstinate little globules.

In a serving bowl, mix the mustard and ginger with the juice of half a lemon till smooth, then add the juice of a whole orange, the port and redcurrant mixture, and finally the little strips of orange and lemon peel. Mix well – it is now ready for use. Cumberland Sauce is always served cold. Stored in a screw-top jar in a cool place, it will keep for several weeks.

Hawaian Ham Steaks

Ingredients for two people:

2 thick slices bread (from a rounded bloomer loaf, if you want to get exactly the right shape)	4 oz Cheddar cheese
	2 pineapple rings, well-drained and wiped
	Freshly milled black pepper
2 smoked English ham steaks	Butter
2 teaspoons made mustard	2 sprigs watercress

First, pre-heat the grill. Cut two thick slices of bread and toast them on both sides. Once toasted, spread one side thickly with butter, then place a ham steak on each buttered slice. Now spread each steak with mustard, cut the cheese into slices and arrange the slices over the ham.

Next, screw some black pepper over the cheese, then pop the pineapple ring on top. Now, put a piece of foil over the grid in the grill pan (to catch any cheese that bubbles over), then put the toast, etc., on the foil and grill until the cheese is bubbling and slightly brown. Serve garnished with sprigs of watercress, accompanied by a green salad, if you have the time and inclination.

Spaghetti alla Carbonara

For four medium appetites or six smaller ones:

1 lb spaghetti	4 egg yolks
3 oz butter	¼ pint single cream
1 tablespoon oil	Freshly grated Parmesan
1 medium onion, finely chopped	Salt and freshly milled black pepper
6 oz back bacon (with rinds removed), cut into small strips	

Bring a very large saucepan of salted water to the boil, and boil the spaghetti for about 10 or 11 minutes or until cooked but slightly underdone – *al dente*, as the Italians say. Meanwhile, sauté the onion in the butter and oil till soft but not browned, and then add the strips of bacon and cook those for a further 5 minutes.

In a small basin, blend the egg yolks and cream together thoroughly. When the spaghetti is cooked, drain it well in a colander, then immediately return it to the dry hot saucepan (not over a heat though), pour over the bacon and onion mixture followed by the cream and egg yolks. Toss thoroughly, then taste a bit and season with salt and freshly milled black pepper. Serve immediately on hot plates with some Parmesan to sprinkle over.

6 Poultry and Game

I can remember a time when chicken was a luxury food, more expensive than meat and proudly offered up only on special occasions. Nowadays chicken is cheap and cheerful – you have only to walk down any high street to see rows of naked carcases rotating in a window, or cartonfuls being rushed off home for re-heating. It is becoming the fish'n chips of the 1970s, but sadly it just is not the same, and the memory of what chicken should taste like grows dimmer with every year. Even to mention the word 'free-range' would be unrealistic.

Quite reasonably the housewife wants the cheapest food possible and the fact that 80 per cent of all chickens sold are frozen shows how willing the industry is to accommodate her. But the choice is a tough one: cheap chicken which is tasteless, or a chicken with flavour which is expensive? Up to a point we still do have a choice. The best-flavoured chicken is undoubtedly the one bought from the family butcher, the sort that's allowed to hang complete with head, feet and innards, and which is drawn only at point of purchase.

The worst sort of chicken is the one off the production line, eviscerated quickly, then plunged into a trough of iced water to be cooled rapidly. At the same time it absorbs up to 10 per cent of its own weight in water and then is packed off to be deep-frozen, water and all. There is fortunately an alternative to water-cooling, and that is air-cooling. With this method no water is absorbed to increase weight or extract flavour, and is why the fresh-chilled chickens don't have the generally seen bleached white look; they have that healthy pinkish tinge you find on fresh chickens hanging in the butcher's. Air-cooled birds are more expensive than frozen but they are well worth it, particularly for plain roasting, if you can't get a plump, freshly drawn one.

Chicken in Cider

To serve four people:

3½-lb chicken, cut into eight
small joints
½ lb dark-gilled mushrooms,
sliced
6 rashers unsmoked streaky
bacon
2 mediun onions, chopped
1 pint dry cider

1 oz butter
1 oz plain flour
1 clove garlic, chopped
1 bay leaf
1 level teaspoon dried mixed
herbs
Oil
Salt and pepper

Pre-heat the oven to gas mark 4 (350°F).

First, fry the chicken pieces in oil to brown, arrange them in a
fireproof casserole, and season with salt and freshly milled black
pepper. Now fry the onions and garlic for 5 minutes or so and
spoon them over the chicken. Next the bacon, which should be
fried to melt a little, then put with the rest in the casserole.
Sprinkle in the herbs, throw in the bay leaf, and add the cider.

Bring it all to simmering point on top of the stove, then replace
the lid and let it simmer for 1 hour. At the end of that time add
the mushrooms and simmer for a further 5 minutes.

Have ready 1 oz plain flour mixed to a smooth paste with 1 oz
butter, and when the chicken is cooked transfer the pieces to a
serving dish, using a draining spoon. Divide the butter and flour
mixture into peanut-sized pieces, toss them into the liquid and
bring back to simmering point, stirring all the time.

Pour the thickened sauce over the chicken and serve immediately with boiled rice.

Chicken Curry

Ingredients for four people:

3½-lb chicken, cut into eight
small joints
1 tablespoon seasoned flour
2 tablespoons olive oil
1 tablespoon butter
2 medium-sized onions,
chopped small
1 large green pepper, chopped

1 clove garlic, crushed
2 level teaspoons Madras curry
powder
1 large tin Italian tomatoes
(15–16 oz)
2 tablespoons natural yoghurt
Salt and freshly milled black
pepper

Heat the butter and oil in a large fireproof casserole, coat the chicken joints in the seasoned flour and fry them to a good golden colour on both sides.

Remove the joints and keep them by while you now gently fry the onion, green pepper and crushed garlic, which will take about 10 minutes. Then add the curry powder, followed by the contents of the tin of tomatoes. Put the chicken joints back in and stir. Season with salt and freshly milled black pepper.

Now on with the lid and simmer for about 40 minutes, or until the chicken is tender. Just before serving stir in the yoghurt. Serve with boiled rice.

Chicken with Lemon Sauce

Quantities for four people:

3½-lb chicken (with giblets)
3 oz softened butter
¼ teaspoon dried tarragon
1 dessertspoon lemon juice
1 lemon, quartered
Salt and freshly milled black
  pepper

for the sauce:
2 oz butter
1 tablespoon flour
¼ pint stock (made with the
  giblets)
1 tablespoon lemon juice
¼ pint double cream

Pre-heat the oven to gas mark 6 (400°F).

First, in a small basin, mix 3 oz butter with ¼ teaspoon salt and 1 dessertspoon lemon juice. Add some dried tarragon and pepper, then spread this mixture all over the breast of the chicken. Cut the lemon into quarters and place the quarters inside the chicken. Place the chicken in a roasting tin, and roast it for 1 to 1¼ hours, basting now and then with the juices.

About 10 minutes before the chicken is ready prepare the sauce. Melt 2 oz butter in a small saucepan, stir in the flour, then gradually stir in the chicken stock and lemon juice. Bring to the boil, stirring all the time, simmer for 2 or 3 minutes, then add the cream and some juice from the chicken. Serve the chicken with the sauce poured over.

Mustard Coated Chicken

For four people:

8 small chicken joints
2 tablespoons German
 mustard
1 tablespoon Dijon mustard
2 egg yolks
2 tablespoons double cream

5 oz dry white breadcrumbs
Flour
Salt and freshly milled black
 pepper
Cooking oil

Begin by removing the skins from the chicken joints, then in a small basin blend together smoothly both the mustards, the egg yolks and the cream. Now take two squares of greaseproof paper: on one place the breadcrumbs, and on the other some flour. Season each chicken joint with salt and freshly milled black pepper, dust with flour, then dip each one first into the mustard mixture (making sure it is evenly coated) then in the breadcrumbs, rolling them and patting the crumbs on firmly.

Place all the joints on a large plate and chill for 3 or 4 hours (so that the mustard flavours can develop and the coating has a chance to become firm).

To cook the chicken you will need either a very large frying pan or two smaller ones with about 1 inch of oil heated to the point where a small cube of bread froths on contact. Fry the chicken joints over a medium heat for about 20 minutes in all, turning them occasionally – they should be crisp and golden.

Drain on kitchen paper and serve hot.

Chicken Paprika

For four people:

4 chicken portions
2 medium onions, sliced
1 medium green pepper, cut
 into small strips
1 large (16 oz) tin Italian
 tomatoes
¼ pint chicken stock

1 dessertspoon flour
1 heaped tablespoon paprika
5-oz carton soured cream
Cooking oil
Salt and pepper

Pre-heat the oven to gas mark 3 (325° F).

Gently fry the chicken joints to a golden colour, then transfer them from the frying pan into a casserole, and season with salt and pepper.

Now, fry the onions gently for about 10 minutes to soften; stir in the flour and paprika, followed by the contents of the tin of tomatoes. Still stirring, add the stock, bring the whole lot to simmering point, then pour over the chicken joints.

Put a lid on the casserole and place in the pre-heated oven. Leave it there for 45 minutes, then add the chopped pepper, stir it in a bit, put the lid back on and let the whole lot cook for a further 30 minutes.

Just before serving, spoon the soured cream all over, mix it in a bit and sprinkle on a little more paprika. Serve with Onion Rice (see p. 153).

Chicken Risotto with Peppers

To serve two people:

1 lb cooked chicken, diced	¾ teacup long-grain rice
1 large green pepper, de-seeded and chopped	2 teacups chicken stock
1 large onion, sliced	Butter
1 clove garlic, chopped	Cooking oil
¼ lb mushrooms	Salt and freshly milled black pepper
8-oz tin Italian tomatoes, drained	

Pre-heat the oven to gas mark 4 (350° F).

First, heat the butter and oil and fry the onions, pepper and garlic in it for about 10 minutes. Then add the stalks of the mushrooms and cook them for a minute or so. Finally, adding the chicken pieces, rice and some pepper and salt, stir with a wooden spoon to blend evenly.

Then transfer everything into a casserole, pour in the hot stock, put the lid on and cook in the oven for about 30 minutes (or until the rice is tender). Just before serving, fry the mushroom caps in a little butter, then add the tomatoes.

Heat through and serve the risotto garnished with the tomatoes and mushrooms.

Chicken Salad with Tarragon and Green Grapes

For four people:

1 cooked chicken (about 2¾ to 3 lb)
¼ pint mayonnaise
3 fl. oz double cream
¼ lb green grapes, peeled and pipped
Lettuce leaves
1 tablespoon fresh chopped tarragon
2 or 3 spring onions, finely chopped
Watercress
Salt and freshly milled black pepper

Remove the skin from the chicken and slice the flesh into longish pieces where possible, then remove all the chicken from the bones and place all the meat in a bowl. Season the chicken with salt and freshly milled black pepper.

In a separate bowl, mix the mayonnaise (see p. 161) thoroughly with the cream, adding the chopped tarragon and spring onions. Now pour this sauce over the chicken, mix it well so that all the chicken pieces get a good coating, then arrange it on a plate of crisp lettuce leaves and garnish with green grapes and a few sprigs of watercress.

Spiced Chicken

To serve four people:

3½-lb freshly drawn chicken, cut into 4 pieces
2 medium onions, chopped small
1 level dessertspoon ground turmeric
1 level dessertspoon ground ginger
1 level teaspoon Madras curry powder
1 clove garlic, crushed
1 tablespoon oil
1½ oz butter
5-oz carton natural yoghurt
5-oz carton single cream
Salt and freshly milled black pepper
Watercress
Mango chutney

A few hours before the meal arrange the chicken pieces side by side in a large shallow casserole that has a lid (or use a meat roasting tin covered with foil). Season the chicken with salt and freshly milled black pepper, then mix the powdered spices together and sprinkle about 1 heaped teaspoonful over the chicken.

Now put a little bit of crushed garlic on each chicken piece, followed by a trickle of oil, and using your hands rub the spices, oil and garlic into the chicken flesh. Then, pierce each portion in several places with a skewer so that all the flavour can permeate them. Leave the chicken in a cool place for several hours to absorb the flavours.

When you are ready to start cooking, pre-heat the oven to gas mark 4 (350°F), then put a small fleck of butter on each chicken joint, and place the casserole in the oven (uncovered) for 30 minutes. Meanwhile fry the onions very gently in a little butter and oil for 10 minutes to soften them, and mix the remaining spices together with the yoghurt and cream.

Take the chicken out of the oven when the 30 minutes are up. Spoon the onion all over them, then pour the yoghurt mixture over, put a lid on or cover with foil and return the chicken to the oven for another 30 to 45 minutes, or until the chicken is tender. Baste once or twice during the cooking, taking the cover off for the last 10 minutes. Serve with Spiced Rice (see p. 153) and mango chutney, with sprigs of watercress as a garnish.

Chicken with Tarragon

For four people:

3½-lb roasting chicken	1 heaped teaspoon flour and ½ oz
2 tablespoons fresh chopped tarragon	butter, combined to a paste
3 oz butter	Salt and freshly milled black pepper
¼ pint single cream	

Pre-heat the oven to gas mark 6 (400°F).

First, mix 1 tablespoon chopped tarragon with 3 oz butter, and season the butter with salt and freshly milled black pepper. Put half the butter mixture inside the chicken; the other half should be used to coat the outside of the chicken thickly all over.

Now, wrap the chicken (not too tightly) in a double sheet of buttered foil, place it on its side in a roasting tin and cook it for 1½ hours – turning it over on to its other side half-way through. When the chicken is cooked, unwrap the foil and pour all the juices into a small saucepan and (while you keep the chicken warm) add the butter and flour paste in small, peanut-sized pieces.

Stir over a low heat till thickened, then add the cream and the rest of the tarragon, allow it to heat through and serve the sauce with the chicken.

Coq au Vin

For four people:

3½-lb chicken, cut into joints	1 or 2 sprigs fresh thyme
½ lb unsmoked streaky bacon (in one piece)	2 tablespoons brandy
	1 bottle red burgundy
16 button onions, peeled	1½ tablespoon butter
½ lb smallish dark-gilled mushrooms	1½ tablespoon plain flour
	Butter, oil
1 large clove garlic, crushed	Salt and freshly milled black
2 bay leaves	pepper

First, melt some butter and oil in a large frying pan and fry the chicken joints, skin side down, until they are a nice golden colour; then turn them over and colour them on the other side (if your frying pan is not very large, do them three or four at a time because to do this properly the pan should not be over-crowded).

Remove the joints from the pan, using a draining spoon, and place them in a large cooking pot.

Now, cut the bacon (rind removed) into smallish cubes, brown them in the frying pan and add them to the chicken, then finally brown the onions a little and add them. Next, place a crushed clove of garlic and a sprig of thyme down into the centre of the chicken pieces, season with freshly milled black pepper but only very little salt (because of the bacon), and throw in a couple of bay leaves.

Place the pot over a medium heat. Warm a ladle and pour the brandy into it: hold the ladle over some heat to warm the brandy, then set light to it and pour over the chicken, rotating the pan to spread the flames.

When the flames have died down, pour in the wine, bring to simmering point, put on a lid and simmer very gently for 45 minutes to 1 hour, or until the chicken is tender.

During the last 15 minutes add the mushrooms and stir them down into the liquid. Finally, remove the chicken, bacon, onions and mushrooms on to a warm serving dish (discarding the bay leaves and thyme at this point), keep warm, then mix the butter and flour to a smooth paste and add it to the liquid in peanut-sized pieces. Bring the liquid to simmering point, by which time the flour and butter will have melted and thickened the sauce.

Pour the sauce over the chicken, and serve with Onion Rice (see p. 153).

Roast Duck with Port and Cherries

For four people:

1 large duck (5 to 6 lb)	½ lb Morello cherry jam
Salt and freshly milled black pepper	¼ pint port
	Watercress

Pre-heat the oven to gas mark 7 (425°F).

Place the duck in a meat roasting tin, then prick the fleshy parts with a skewer and sprinkle it quite generously with freshly milled black pepper and salt. Add nothing else whatever – no fat, butter, etc. – just place the tin on a high shelf in the oven, then, after about 25 minutes, turn the heat down to gas mark 5 (375°F), and cook it for a further 3 hours. This long cooking will ensure that the duck is crisp and free of fat. During the cooking, take out the roasting tin two or three times and pour off the fat (which, by the way, is very good for roast potatoes).

The sauce takes only about 10 minutes from start to finish. Simply combine the jam with the port in a saucepan and simmer it gently for about 8 minutes.

To serve the duck, chop it into four quarters with a sharp knife or kitchen scissors. Arrange the quarters on a serving dish, pour the sauce over and garnish with a few sprigs of watercress.

(Note: The jam must be Morello cherry – no other cherry jam will do.)

Roast Duck with Bigarade Sauce

As an alternative to the above recipe, when Seville oranges are in season, make a sauce with:

2 smallish Seville oranges	3 heaped teaspoons brown sugar
½ pint stock, made with duck giblets	1 rounded tablespoon flour
4 or 5 tablespoons port	Salt and pepper

First, thinly pare off the outer rinds of the oranges – a potato peeler is good for this – cut the rinds into tiny shreds and blanch them in boiling water for about 5 minutes, then drain well. Now squeeze the juice out of the oranges, and reserve it.

When the duck is cooked, remove it to a serving plate, cut it into quarters and keep warm in the oven. Then place the roasting tin over a medium heat and sprinkle in 1 tablespoon flour. Work it into the duck juices to form a smooth paste, cook it for a minute or two to brown lightly (scraping the base and sides of the tin with a wooden spoon), then add the stock a little at a time to make a smooth sauce.

Add the sugar, cook it for a minute or two, then add the orange juice and rinds and a seasoning of salt and pepper. Just before serving, add the port. Pour the sauce over the duck and serve immediately.

GAME

Guinea Fowl

For two or four people (the meat is quite rich):

1 guinea fowl (approx. 1½ lb)
2 oz butter
1 small onion, finely chopped

2 juniper berries, crushed
Salt and pepper

for the stuffing:
1 oz white breadcrumbs
4 oz unsmoked streaky bacon, chopped
1 egg yolk beaten with 4 tablespoons milk
3 tablespoons fresh chopped parsley
4 juniper berries, crushed
Salt and pepper

for the sauce:
¼ pint red burgundy
1 tablespoon port
1 dessertspoon redcurrant jelly
1 dessertspoon flour
¼ pint stock

Pre-heat the oven to gas mark 7 (425°F).

First, wipe the guinea fowl inside and out. To make the stuffing, combine all the ingredients (it should be fairly soft, if not add another drop of milk). Now pack the stuffing into the body cavity of the bird and place a small skewer in the gap to close it. Next, combine the softened butter with the chopped onion and crushed juniper berries, adding salt and pepper.

Smear this all over the bird, then place it in a small roasting tin and roast for about 50 minutes, basting frequently. To tell when the bird is cooked, pierce the thickest part of the flesh between body and thigh and if the juices run clear and it feels tender, it is ready. Now remove the trussing and skewer and place the bird on a serving dish, cover and keep warm.

To make the sauce, drain the clear fat from the pan juices, place the pan over direct heat, add 1 dessertspoon flour, blending it in with a wooden spoon. Gradually pour in the burgundy and stir, scraping the base and sides of the pan to dislodge all the nice crusty bits.

Now reduce the heat to low and pour in the port, redcurrant jelly and stock. Simmer for 2 or 3 minutes then taste to check the seasoning, and serve the bird with the sauce separately.

Casserole of Pheasant

To serve three or four people:

1 pheasant, plucked and trussed
Salt and freshly milled black pepper
1 onion, chopped
1 tablespoon butter
1 tablespoon oil
½ pint good red wine

½ tablespoon butter and ½ tablespoon flour, combined to a paste
2 teaspoons sugar
8 button onions, peeled and left whole
8 button mushrooms, left whole
Chicken stock

Pre-heat the oven to gas mark 2 (300°F).

Wipe the pheasant inside and out, then stuff the body cavity with the chopped onion (and the bird's liver, if available), and season inside and out.

Then in a deep wide pan heat 1 tablespoon each of butter and oil together and brown the bird all over in the hot fat, and transfer it to an ovenproof casserole. Pour the wine into the pan and heat, scraping the base and sides of pan. Allow the wine to boil until reduced by half, then remove from the heat.

Stir in small pieces of the butter and flour mixture, then return the pan to the heat and bring to the boil, stirring briskly. Add the sugar, then pour the sauce over the pheasant in the casserole.

Simmer the button onions in salted water for 5 minutes, then add them to the casserole together with the mushrooms. Bring the contents of the casserole to simmering point, then cover and bake in the oven, basting occasionally (if the sauce shows signs of cooking away too quickly, add a tablespoon or two of chicken stock).

A young and tender pheasant will be done in 40 to 45 minutes; an older bird may take up to 2 hours to cook.

When ready to serve, remove the trussing, drain well and place on a heated serving dish. Skim the pan juices (if necessary), taste and season, surround the pheasant with the onions and mushrooms and spoon the sauce over the bird.

Old English Rabbit Pie

To serve four people:

1 largish rabbit (approx. 3 lb), cut into joints

2 medium onions, chopped fairly small

½ lb unsmoked streaky bacon (one piece)

1 medium cooking apple, peeled and sliced

¼ lb dried prunes, pitted (weighed after extracting the stones)

½ pint dry cider

¾ pint stock (or water)

½ whole nutmeg, grated

1 bay leaf

1½ oz plain flour and 1½ oz butter (combined to a smooth paste)

Salt and freshly milled black pepper

Suet crust pastry (see below)

Pre-heat the oven to gas mark 7 (425°F).

First, wash the rabbit joints and place them in a large saucepan (no need to include the ribs as there is not enough meat on them). Tuck the chopped onion and apple in amongst the joints, then take the rind off the bacon, chop the meat into 1-inch cubes and add it to the rabbit. Now throw in a bay leaf, a little salt and plenty of freshly milled black pepper. Pour in the cider and stock, bring it to simmering point, skim off any bits of scum that may have appeared, then cover and leave to simmer gently for about 1 hour or until the rabbit is tender.

Next, remove the rabbit, bacon, apple and onion (using a draining spoon) and transfer to a pie dish – a 2½-pint oval dish would be ideal – then sprinkle in the chopped prunes. To the stock left in the saucepan add the butter and flour mixture in peanut-sized pieces, and stir them over a medium heat to melt and thicken the sauce. Add the freshly grated nutmeg, and when it reaches simmering point pour the sauce over the rabbit.

Now make a suet crust pastry using:

12 oz self-raising flour
6 oz shredded suet
Cold water, to mix

½ teaspoon salt
Freshly milled black pepper

Mix the flour, salt, pepper and suet together, and add enough cold water to make a fairly soft elastic dough that leaves the bowl cleanly. Roll it out about 1 inch wider than the pie dish, and cut a 1-inch wide piece all round. Dampen the edges of the dish and press the strip all round the rim of the dish. Now dampen the rim of pastry and put the rest of the pastry lid on, pressing well all round to seal the edges.

Decorate the edges with fluting, if you like; make a small hole in the centre to allow steam to escape, and bake in the hot oven for 30 minutes, or until the crust is golden-brown.

(Note: this suet pastry must be made with self-raising flour – using plain flour will cause the pastry to become very hard.)

Rabbit in Red Wine

To serve four people:

2 lb rabbit joints or 1 medium rabbit, jointed
1 oz butter
1 tablespoon oil
½ lb unsmoked streaky bacon (bought in one piece and cubed, or failing that, roughly chopped rashers), with rind removed
2 medium onions, chopped
1 level tablespoon flour
½ pint red wine
¼ pint stock
½ lb dark-gilled mushrooms, sliced
1 clove garlic, crushed
1 sprig fresh thyme or ½ teaspoon dried
Salt, freshly milled black pepper

Heat the butter and the oil in a large, flameproof casserole, then fry the rabbit joints quickly to brown them nicely all over.

Remove them on to a plate, then fry the onions, garlic and bacon for approximately 10 minutes. Now sprinkle in the flour, stir it around, cook it for a minute or two, then gradually stir in the red wine and the stock.

Add the rabbit joints at this point and the thyme. Bring everything to simmering point, then add the sliced mushrooms, together with a seasoning of salt and freshly milled black pepper. Then, cover and simmer very gently for 1 hour, or until the rabbit is tender.

When the rabbit is cooked, remove it to a serving dish, together with the onions and mushrooms, then boil the remaining liquid briskly to reduce it slightly. When the sauce is reduced pour it over the rabbit and serve.

(Note: White wine could equally well be used, or dry cider with a sliced apple added to the onions.)

Roasted Rabbit with Onions, Bacon and Forcemeat

To serve four:

1 largish rabbit, jointed
2 large onions, peeled and
  chopped
½ lb fat streaky bacon
1½ tablespoons seasoned flour
Dripping or butter
Salt and freshly milled black
  pepper

for the forcemeat:
½ lb pork sausage-meat
½ teaspoon dried sage
1 level tablespoon fresh
  chopped parsley
½ smallish onion, grated or
  chopped very small
Salt and freshly milled black
  pepper
Nutmeg

Pre-heat the oven to gas mark 4 (350°F).

Dust the rabbit joints with seasoned flour and wrap each joint in one or two rashers of streaky bacon. Now arrange them in a roasting tin, season with freshly milled black pepper and just a little salt (because there is some in the bacon).

Tuck the pieces of onion in and around the rabbit (putting some pieces underneath the joints), then dot with little knobs of dripping here and there, using about 2 oz in all. Place the roasting tin in the oven and cook for 1 hour, basting with the fat and juices at least three times, before adding the forcemeat.

To make the forcemeat, mix the sausage-meat, sage, onion and parsley together. Season well with salt and freshly milled black pepper, then add a good grating of nutmeg. Now take teaspoonfuls of this mixture and roll them into balls. Dust them with the remainder of the flour, and after the rabbit has cooked for an hour add them to it. Baste with hot fat and cook for a further 30 minutes.

Finally, remove everything to a serving dish, spoon off the fat from the roasting tin, and make a gravy to go with the rabbit.

7 Offal

No one cares for the undignified word 'offal', especially me. So I always refer to liver, kidneys, sweetbreads etc. as 'spare parts', and it is my considered opinion that they are going to play a much larger part in our day-to-day diet in future, if only because of the ever-increasing costs of meat. Liver and kidneys are not cheap by any means, but since we need a smaller quantity (1 lb can quite adequately feed four people) they do in practice work out more economical than other cuts. And as an added bonus, they are also so rich in essential nutrients that nutritionalists would have us all eat one or another at least once a week.

Kidneys in Jacket Potatoes

For this supper dish for four you will need 4 large potatoes, and they usually take 1 to $1\frac{1}{2}$ hours to bake in the oven at gas mark 6 (400° F).

When you have washed them it is very important to dry them again very thoroughly so that the skins will turn nice and crisp during the cooking. Place them on a baking sheet on a high shelf in the oven. The rest of the ingredients are:

4 lambs' kidneys, skinned and
  with the core removed
8 rashers bacon
Made-up French or English
  mustard

2 oz butter
Salt and freshly milled black
  pepper

When the potatoes are cooked, hold them with a cloth and cut them into halves and in four of the halves make a depression with the back of a tablespoon. Season and put a knob of butter in each.

Now spread the kidneys with a little mustard and wrap each one in two rashers of bacon. Place them in the buttered halves on the potatoes and return them to the oven for about 20 minutes, keeping the other halves warm. To serve, place the potato halves together again.

Kidney and Bacon Risotto

Serves four people:

1 lb lambs' kidneys
2 oz butter
2 tablespoons oil
1 Spanish onion, chopped
1 clove garlic, crushed
6 oz long-grain rice
14-oz tin Italian tomatoes
¼ pint stock (made from a cube)

6 slices back bacon, chopped small
¼ lb dark-gilled mushrooms, thinly sliced
Salt and freshly milled black pepper
1 bay leaf
¼ teaspoon dried oregano
Parsley, chopped

Skin the kidneys, slice them in half and snip out the cores with a pair of scissors. Now heat 1 oz of butter and 1 tablespoon of oil in a saucepan and gently soften the onion and garlic in it for about 10 minutes. Next, stir in the rice and pour in the contents of the tin of tomatoes and the stock, plus a bay leaf and ¼ teaspoon oregano. Add a little seasoning, stir just once, then put a lid on and let it simmer gently for 20 to 25 minutes, or until the rice is tender and most of the liquid has been absorbed.

Meanwhile, gently fry the bacon in the rest of the butter and oil, then turn the heat up, add the halved kidneys and cook them for 3 to 4 minutes (turning them frequently). Add the sliced mushrooms and cook for a further 4 minutes (the kidneys should be pink inside).

Taste the rice mixture when it is ready, season if necessary, and serve the rice arranged on a warmed serving plate, with the kidneys and bacon and their juice spooned over. Sprinkle with parsley and serve.

Kidneys Stroganoff

For four people:

8 lambs' kidneys
3 level tablespoons butter
1 medium onion, chopped small
½ lb mushrooms, thinly sliced through the stalks

5-oz carton soured cream
Freshly grated nutmeg
Salt and freshly milled black pepper

Cut the kidneys in half and, with a pair of scissors, cut out the cores, then slice each half in two. Heat 2 tablespoons butter in a frying pan and gently fry the onion and mushrooms till soft – about 10 minutes – then remove from the pan (using a draining spoon) and keep warm. Add another tablespoon of butter to the pan, then gently fry the kidneys, turning them now and then, for about 8 to 10 minutes or until they are tender but still pink inside.

Now add the mushrooms and onions, stir them around for a few minutes, then keeping the heat fairly low stir in the soured cream and allow it to heat through. Season with salt and freshly milled black pepper and freshly grated nutmeg.

Serve with rice or buttered noodles, and a crisp green salad.

Stuffed Lambs' Kidneys

For three people:

6 lambs' kidneys	4 tablespoons soured cream
1 onion, finely chopped	2 tablespoons dry sherry
5 tablespoons fresh white breadcrumbs	2 tablespoons chicken stock
2 tablespoons fresh chopped parsley	Butter
	Salt and freshly milled black pepper
1 level teaspoon fresh chopped thyme (or ½ teaspoon dried)	6 thin bacon rashers

Pre-heat the oven to gas mark 7 (425°F).

Skin the kidneys, split them in half lengthways without separating the two halves completely, then using a pair of scissors, snip away the cores. Melt about 2 level tablespoons of butter in a frying pan and fry the chopped onion till softened, then remove from the heat and stir in the breadcrumbs and herbs, season with salt and freshly milled black pepper, and add 1 tablespoon soured cream to bind the mixture together.

Now pile this mixture into the kidneys and wrap each one round with a thin rasher of bacon, and place the kidneys in a buttered roasting tin; dot with a bit more butter and bake near the top of the oven for 15 minutes.

Remove them from the tin and place on a warmed serving dish

and keep warm. Now put the roasting tin over a very gentle heat, stir the sherry and chicken stock into the juices, finally adding the soured cream. Pour the sauce over the kidneys and serve.

Kidneys in Fresh Tomato Sauce

For two people:

6 lambs' kidneys, skinned, cored and cut into halves	1 tablespoon tomato purée
	Olive oil
¾ lb ripe red tomatoes	1 level dessertspoon flour
1 medium onion, finely chopped	Salt and freshly milled black pepper
1 clove garlic, crushed	
¼ teaspoon dried basil	

In a medium-sized saucepan cook the onions and garlic gently in some olive oil for about 6 minutes. Meanwhile pour boiling water on the tomatoes and after a few minutes slip the skins off and chop the flesh roughly (discarding most of the seeds). Now add the kidneys to the onions, turn the heat up slightly and brown the kidneys, stirring and turning them around. Next sprinkle in the flour, cook that for a minute or two, then add the chopped tomatoes, tomato purée and basil. Have another good stir, season well with salt and freshly milled black pepper, then put a lid on the saucepan and simmer over a gentle heat for about 20 minutes.

Serve with either buttered noodles or rice.

Kidneys in Red Wine

To serve three people:

6 small lambs' kidneys	1 level teaspoon flour
1 large onion, chopped	¼ teaspoon dried thyme
¾ lb dark-gilled mushrooms	½ pint red wine
4 rashers unsmoked bacon, chopped	2 oz dripping or butter
	Salt, freshly milled black pepper
1 clove garlic, crushed	

Melt the fat in a largish saucepan and gently fry the onion and garlic in it for about 5 minutes, then add the bacon and mushrooms and cook for a further 10 minutes. Meanwhile prepare the kidneys by cutting them in half, pulling the skins off and snipping the cores out with kitchen scissors.

Add the kidneys to the other ingredients in the saucepan, and let them colour a little (stirring them around). Then stir in the flour to soak up the juices, sprinkle in the thyme, and gradually add the wine. Bring to simmering point, season with freshly milled black pepper and just a little salt (because the bacon is salty). Put a lid on the saucepan and simmer gently for about 20 to 25 minutes. Taste to check the seasoning and serve with Onion Rice (see p. 153).

(Note: Cube beef stock can be used instead of wine, or even an 8-oz tin of Italian tomatoes with 2 tablespoons water added.)

Gougère with Chicken Livers

To serve three people:

for the pastry:
¼ pint water
2 oz butter
2½ oz plain flour
2 eggs
2 oz grated Cheddar
Salt and pepper

for the filling:
1 oz butter
1 level tablespoon flour
8 oz chicken livers
1 medium onion, sliced
¼ lb mushrooms, sliced
1 tomato, skinned and chopped
¼ pint stock
1 tablespoon grated Cheddar cheese
1 tablespoon chopped parsley

Pre-heat the oven to gas mark 6 (400°F).

Begin by putting the water and butter into a large pan and bring to the boil, then take it off the heat, pour in the flour and beat as vigorously as you can until the mixture is smooth (and leaves the side of the pan). Beat in the eggs, then the cheese, and continue beating for 3 minutes. Season with pepper and salt, then set aside.

Melt ½ oz butter in a pan and sauté the livers for 5 minutes, then remove. Add the remaining butter and soften the onions in it (10 minutes); add the sliced mushrooms, then blend in 1 level tablespoon flour. Stir in the stock, season with salt and pepper, and simmer for 5 minutes. Take the pan off the heat and add the livers and tomatoes.

Now take a well-greased oval baking dish (about 10 in. in length), arrange the cheese paste all round the border leaving a hollow in the centre, pour the filling into the centre, sprinkle grated cheese all over, and bake in the oven for 30 to 40 minutes, by which time the paste will have risen and be golden-brown.

Sprinkle with chopped parsley and serve immediately.

Liver with Pepper and Paprika Sauce

For two people:

½ lb lamb's liver	1 heaped teaspoon paprika
1 small green pepper	6 tablespoons red wine
1 small onion	Salt and freshly milled black
¼ pint soured cream	pepper
2 oz butter	

Chop the onion quite small, de-seed the pepper and cut it into small, thin strips (about 1 inch in length). Prepare the liver with a sharp knife by cutting it into smallish strips (again about 1 inch long). Melt the butter in a frying pan and gently soften the onion in it for about 5 minutes, then add the pepper and cook that for about 5 minutes or so.

Turn the heat up, add the pieces of liver and a good seasoning of salt and freshly milled black pepper. Turn the liver over to brown it nicely all over, then add the wine. Let it bubble for a few seconds then take the pan off the heat and stir in the soured cream and paprika. Return the pan to the heat (lowered a little) and bring the whole lot to simmering point. Taste to check the seasoning.

Serve with rice cooked with onion and chopped pepper.

Peppered Liver

For two people:

¾ lb lamb's liver (ask the butcher to cut it into very thin slices)	1 dessertspoon olive oil
	1 teaspoon butter
	½ glass red or white wine
2 teaspoons whole black peppercorns	1 level teaspoon salt
1 tablespoon flour	

First of all, you need to crush the peppercorns. Ideally, this should be done with a pestle and mortar, but you can do it with the back of a tablespoon on a flat surface – provided you are prepared to crawl around on all fours retrieving the ones that jump off.

When the peppercorns are crushed (coarsely) add them to the flour with a level teaspoon of salt, then dip the pieces of liver in it, pressing the pepper in a bit on both sides. In a large frying pan, heat the oil and butter, put the liver slices in and cook them very gently for a minute or two.

When the blood starts to run, turn them over and gently cook them on the other side for slightly less time (they must not on any account be over-cooked).

Transfer them on to a warm serving dish, add ½ glass wine to the pan – let it bubble and reduce, then pour it over the liver. Serve with creamy mashed potatoes.

Stuffed Liver and Bacon

For four people:

4 slices lamb's liver (about ½ inch thick), about 1 lb in all	1 level dessertspoon shredded suet
4 rashers short back bacon (rinds removed)	¼ pint boiling water
½ packet sage and onion stuffing (approx. 2 oz)	1 tablespoon well-seasoned flour
	1 oz dripping

Pre-heat the oven to gas mark 4 (350°F).

Put the dripping in a roasting tin and leave it in the oven to melt. Now wipe the liver and coat each piece in the seasoned flour. Make up the stuffing using ¼ pint boiling water, add the suet, mixing well, then spoon the stuffing on to the pieces of liver – spreading it all over.

Place a rasher of bacon on each one (pressing it on firmly), then using a spatula lift each slice of liver into the meat tin containing the hot fat. Cover with a piece of buttered foil and bake for 20 minutes, then remove the foil and bake for a further 10 minutes.

Venetian Liver

For four people:

4 slices lamb's liver (about ½ inch thick), about 1 lb in all
½ pint red wine
2 medium onions, finely sliced
1½ oz butter

1 level teaspoon powdered oregano
1 level tablespoon flour
Salt and freshly milled black pepper

Arrange the thin slices of liver in a shallow dish, sprinkle with the powdered oregano, pour the wine over and leave it to marinade for 4 to 8 hours. When you are ready to cook the liver, cook the finely sliced onions in butter till soft (about 10–15 minutes). Sprinkle in the flour, cook for a minute or two, then gradually stir in the marinade, bit by bit, to make a smooth sauce (you can add a bit more wine here, if you think it needs it). Now, in another frying pan, cook the liver slices very quickly in hot butter till stiffened, being very careful not to over-cook. Serve the liver with the onion and wine sauce poured over.

Oxtail Casserole

For four people:

1 oxtail (weighing about 2½ lb), cut in sections
2 tablespoons beef dripping
8 small carrots
8 small onions, peeled
4 slices streaky bacon, diced
½ pint beef stock
¼ pint red wine
1 teaspoon Worcestershire sauce

4 juniper berries, crushed
½ teaspoon dried thyme
1 bay leaf
1 oz butter and 1 oz flour (combined together to a paste)
Salt and freshly milled black pepper

Pre-heat the oven to gas mark 3 (325°F).

In a large fireproof casserole, melt the dripping and fry the pieces of oxtail over a fairly high heat until they are evenly browned all over. Now add the prepared vegetables and the bacon and cook these in the hot fat until golden, but not browned.

Now, carefully spoon off the excess fat from the casserole, add the remaining ingredients (except the butter and flour), then bring the contents of the casserole to simmering point, season, then cover and cook in the oven for 3 to 3½ hours (the meat should be falling from the bones).

Using a draining spoon, remove the meat and vegetables to a warm serving dish, then cover and keep warm in the oven. Now boil the remaining pan juices briskly until reduced by about half.

Take the pan off the heat, add the butter and flour mixture in very small pieces, then return to the heat and bring to simmering point, stirring all the time.

Simmer for 2 to 3 minutes, taste to check the seasoning, then pour sauce over the meat and vegetables and serve.

Sweetbread Kebabs

For four people:

1 lb sweetbreads (lambs' or calves')	½ lb unsmoked bacon rashers
1 tablespoon white wine vinegar	A little stock
½ lb small mushroom caps	Salt and freshly milled black pepper

Soak the sweetbreads in cold salted water for 3 hours (or overnight) then drain and rinse well. Place them in a saucepan and cover with a little stock, add some salt and the white wine vinegar, then bring slowly to the boil and simmer gently (3 minutes for lambs' sweetbreads, 10 to 12 minutes for calves').

Now drain the sweetbreads and rinse again with cold water. Remove the outer membranes and any tubes etc., then press the sweetbreads between two plates, weigh them down and chill for about 2 hours.

When you are ready to cook, slice the sweetbreads thickly, then thread alternate pieces of sweetbread and whole mushroom caps on to skewers. Wrap the skewers around with the rashers of bacon, and pre-heat the grill to its highest.

Grill the meat for about 8 minutes, turning the skewers from time to time and basting with the juices. Serve the kebabs with a creamy, garlicky bread sauce.

Tripe and Onions

For four to six people:

2 lb tripe	*to finish off:*
1 large carrot, cut into chunks	1½ oz butter
1 celery stalk, cut into chunks	2 Spanish onions, sliced
1 Spanish onion, quartered	¼ pint double cream
1 bay leaf	¼ pint reduced cooking liquid
1 blade of mace	Lemon juice
A few parsley stalks	Salt and freshly milled black
Salt and pepper	pepper

When you buy the tripe ask the butcher's advice about how much cooking it will need. Cut the tripe into manageable pieces and place in a saucepan with enough cold water to cover, and add the celery, carrots, quartered onion, herbs and seasoning, then put a lid on and simmer for about 30 minutes.

Drain the tripe thoroughly and cut into 1-inch squares. Now boil the cooking liquid to reduce by about one third, and strain it (discarding the vegetables) into a bowl. To finish off, melt the butter in a flameproof casserole and cook the sliced onion in it until softened (10 to 15 minutes), then lay the pieces of tripe on top of the onions, pour over the cream, followed by ¼ pint of the reduced stock.

Put a lid on and cook gently for a further 45 minutes, being careful not to over-cook – it should be tender but still have some 'bite' to it. Squeeze a little lemon juice on before serving.

8 Vegetables and Salads

When it comes to vegetables, I am an undeviating follower of the seasons. I am just not interested in Brussels sprouts in June or fresh tomatoes at Christmas. For a long time now people have mistakenly thought that to buy something right out of season was somehow chic or clever but, as I have pointed out many times in my columns, I think a lot of the tiresome decision-making involved in everyday cooking is due to the fact that absolutely everything is always available.

How much nicer it is to look forward to the first young, tender green peas of early summer, or the incomparable flavour of English celery after a good November frost. Nature *does* provide us with a perfectly varied diet throughout the year, and home-grown vegetables and salads in season are not only far superior to, but cheaper than, those that are imported out of season and have to travel thousands of miles to reach us. (Note: the recipes in this book that contain tomatoes should make use of tinned Italian tomatoes throughout the winter and home-grown fresh tomatoes in the summer.)

Cabbage with Cheese Sauce

For four to six people:

2 lb cabbage (tight green variety)
¾ pint stock
2 tablespoons butter
1 small onion, finely chopped
2 tablespoons flour
½ teaspoon dry mustard
½ pint milk
2 oz sharp Cheddar cheese, grated
Salt and freshly milled black pepper

Pre-heat the oven to gas mark 6 (400°F).

First cut the cabbage into six wedges and remove the hard stalk. Heat the stock in a large saucepan until it boils, put the cabbage sections in, cover and simmer gently for about 10 minutes.

Now melt the butter in a small saucepan and soften the finely chopped onion in it. Stir in the flour and mustard, and cook over a medium heat for a minute or two, before gradually adding the milk (stirring well after each addition). Bring to the boil, still stirring, then simmer for 2 or 3 minutes. Now beat in the cheese and season with salt and pepper.

Drain the cabbage well and arrange in a shallow baking dish. Pour the sauce over the cabbage and bake near the top of the oven for 15 to 20 minutes, or until browned.

White Cabbage with Bacon and Onion

Quantities for two:

1½ lb white cabbage (about half a medium-sized head)
1 clove garlic, crushed
1 medium onion, chopped small

4 bacon rashers, chopped
Olive oil
Salt and freshly milled black pepper

Discard the tough outer leaves of the cabbage; cut it into quarters removing the hard core, then shred reasonably finely. Wash the shredded cabbage in cold water and put into a colander, shaking off any excess moisture.

Gently fry the onions and garlic in oil for 5 minutes (use a saucepan for this), then add the chopped bacon and let that cook for a further 5 minutes.

Finally, add the cabbage, stir it round and round and allow it to cook for 5 or 6 more minutes (shaking the pan from time to time and stirring it round).

Season with freshly milled black pepper, but watch the salt as there is probably some in the bacon.

Baked Spring Cabbage with Juniper Berries

For three or four people:

1½–2 lb spring cabbage	6 juniper berries, crushed
1 onion, finely chopped	Olive oil
2 cloves garlic, finely chopped	Salt, freshly milled black pepper

Pre-heat the oven to gas mark 6 (400°F).

Remove the tough outer leaves of the cabbage and discard them, selecting only the good green leaves. Remove the centres of these, then shred the cabbage very finely. Wash well in a colander and dry thoroughly in a clean cloth or some kitchen paper.

Take a small flameproof casserole, pour in enough olive oil to just cover the bottom and gently fry the onion and garlic in it till pale gold, then stir in the cabbage and juniper berries (which should be crushed finely in a pestle and mortar, or with the back of a tablespoon), plus a seasoning of salt and freshly milled black pepper. Stir to get everything glistening with oil then cover tightly and bake in the oven for 35 minutes, by which time the cabbage will be cooked, but underdone and nice and crisp.

Braised Red Cabbage and Apples

To serve six people:

2 lb red cabbage
1 lb onions, chopped small
1 lb cooking apples, peeled, cored and chopped small
3 tablespoons wine vinegar
3 tablespoons brown sugar
1 garlic clove, chopped very small

¼ whole nutmeg, freshly grated
¼ level teaspoon ground cinnamon
¼ level teaspoon ground cloves
½ oz butter
Salt, freshly milled black pepper

Pre-heat the oven to gas mark 2 (300° F).

Discard the tough outer leaves of the cabbage, cut it into quarters and remove the hard stalk, then shred the cabbage finely. In a fairly large casserole, arrange a layer of shredded cabbage seasoned with salt and pepper, then a layer of chopped onions and apples with a sprinkling of garlic, spices and sugar. Continue with these alternating layers until everything is in.

Now pour in the wine vinegar, add a knob of butter, put a lid on the casserole and let it cook very slowly in the oven for 2½ to 3 hours, stirring everything around once or twice during the cooking. Red cabbage, once cooked, will keep warm without coming to any harm. It will also re-heat very successfully – so it can be made in advance if necessary. Serve it with sausages, or pork dishes, or Lancashire Hotpot (see p. 96).

Cauliflower with Cheese and Onion Sauce

For four people:

1 medium cauliflower
1 bay leaf
1 oz flour
1 small onion, chopped very small

2 oz grated Cheddar cheese
¼ pint milk
2 oz butter
Salt and cayenne pepper

Place the washed cauliflower in a saucepan with about 1 inch of boiling water, some salt and a bay leaf in it. Simmer, with the lid on (10 to 15 minutes) until tender but still firm (it is very important not to over-cook it).

Meanwhile, melt the butter in a small saucepan and soften the onion in it for 5 minutes or so, then add the flour. Stir till smooth, then add the milk a little at a time, stirring vigorously. When the cauliflower is cooked, strain the water into a jug and keep the cauliflower warm in a serving dish. Now add ¼ pint of the cooking water to the onions – gradually, and stirring after each addition – then finally add the grated cheese and a seasoning of salt and cayenne pepper.

Cook the sauce gently for a minute or two, then pour it over the cauliflower and serve immediately.

Courgettes

For two people:

1 lb small young courgettes	Salt and freshly milled black
1½ oz butter	pepper

Wipe the courgettes and, leaving their skins on, cut them into 1-inch rounds, then place them in a colander and sprinkle with salt (about 1 heaped teaspoonful). Next, fit a plate on top of them and weigh it down with a weight or heavy object, and leave them like that for 1 hour or so, so that all the excess moisture can drain out (this is a very easy operation, not half the bother it sounds).

Dry the courgettes, place them in a saucepan with approximately ¼ pint boiling water and simmer them gently for about 8 minutes, then drain. Melt the butter in the same saucepan, add the courgettes and let them cook gently in the butter for a minute or two until tender, moving them around and shaking the pan to prevent them sticking. Season to taste with salt and freshly milled black pepper before serving.

(If you do not have time to prepare the courgettes as above, then place them in a saucepan with the water and butter together, season with salt and simmer till tender).

Petits Pois à la Française

For four people:

2 lb young peas, freshly shelled	2 oz butter
6 lettuce leaves	A pinch of sugar
8 spring onions	Salt

Trim the onions, as you only need the bulbous white part (save the green bits for salads). Break the lettuce leaves into wide strips, then melt the butter in a thick-based saucepan. Add the onions, lettuce and peas, stir well, then add 4 tablespoons water, a pinch of sugar and 1 level teaspoon salt.

Bring to simmering point, then cover the saucepan and let it cook over a very gentle heat for 25 to 30 minutes, but keep an eye on it and shake the pan now and then to prevent the vegetables sticking (and add just a little more water if you think it needs it).

These are delicious served with chops or steaks and buttered new potatoes.

Potatoes Boulangère

To serve four:

2 lb potatoes, sliced	2 oz butter
1 largish onion, finely chopped	Salt, freshly milled black
¼ pint hot stock	pepper
¼ pint milk	

Pre-heat the oven to gas mark 4 (350°F).

The best cooking utensil for this recipe is either an oblong roasting tin or a wide, shallow baking dish. Butter it generously (all over the sides as well), then peel the potatoes and cut them into thinnish slices. Peel the onion and chop it finely.

Now, arrange a layer of potatoes over the base of the tin, followed by a sprinkling of onion and a seasoning of salt and freshly milled black pepper. Continue with another layer of potatoes, and so on until everything is in and you finish up with a layer of potatoes (seasoned) at the top. Pour in the stock and milk and fleck the surface all over with dots of butter.

Place the tin on the highest shelf of the oven, and leave it there for about 45 minutes or until the potatoes are cooked and the top layer is nicely golden-brown. These potatoes will keep warm in a low oven for quite some time without spoiling.

Garlic Stuffed Potatoes

For three people:

3 large potatoes
5-oz packet Boursin cheese
  (with garlic and herbs)
2 oz butter

2 oz grated Cheddar cheese
Oil
Salt and freshly milled black
  pepper

Pre-heat the oven to gas mark 6 (400°F).

Wash the potatoes and dry them thoroughly, then smear the skins with a little olive oil (to help make them crisp). Prick them and place them on the highest oven shelf to bake for 1 to 1½ hours, or until soft. Then, holding each potato in a cloth, slice them in half lengthways and scrape all the inside part into a bowl; add the Boursin, the butter and a good seasoning of salt and pepper, and beat the mixture till smooth, using a fork or an electric whisk.

Finally, pile the mixture back into the empty potato skins, sprinkle with grated Cheddar cheese, and place under a hot grill till the cheese has melted and browned a bit on top.

Jacket Potatoes with Leeks and Bacon

For two people:

2 large potatoes
Olive oil
3 tablespoons single cream
2 oz butter

2 leeks, trimmed, sliced and
  washed
6 rashers smoked back bacon,
  chopped

Wash the potatoes and dry thoroughly, then prick the skins with a fork and smear the outsides with a trace of olive oil (to make them crisp when cooked).

Pre-heat the oven to gas mark 6 (400°F), place the potatoes on the rungs of the highest shelf and bake them for 1 to 1½ hours, or until they feel soft when tested with a skewer. Towards the end of this cooking time, heat about 1 oz butter in a medium-sized saucepan and fry the chopped bacon until it is fairly crisp, then remove it with a draining spoon and keep it warm.

Now add the chopped leeks to the fat remaining in the pan, stir them round until they are coated with butter, then put a lid on and let them cook gently for about 10 minutes.

When the potatoes are ready, halve them and, using a spoon, scrape out all the cooked potato into a bowl. Now add 1 oz butter, 3 tablespoons cream and a good seasoning of salt and freshly milled black pepper. Next, add the chopped bacon and the leeks, plus their buttery pan juices. Mix well, then pile the mixture back into the potato halves. Arrange them on a heatproof dish, and place them under a hot grill until the tops are golden brown.

Jersey Potatoes with Fresh Herbs

For two people:

1 lb fresh Jersey potatoes	1 tablespoon finely chopped
2 oz butter	fresh parsley
1 tablespoon fresh chopped	Salt and freshly milled black
mint	pepper
1 tablespoon fresh snipped	2 large sprigs fresh mint
chives	

Never scrape new Jersey potatoes, otherwise you lose a lot of the flavour – just gently clean them under a cold running tap, rubbing away the dust and specks with your fingers.

Have ready a kettle full of boiling water; place the potatoes in a saucepan with salt and a couple of sprigs of fresh mint. Pour on enough boiling water to come two-thirds of the way up the potatoes, put a tight lid on, and boil them over a medium heat for 20 to 25 minutes (depending on their size), but they must not be over-cooked, or they go soggy. Test them with a thin skewer; they should be just cooked, but still firm.

Drain them well in a colander, then return them to the saucepan with the butter, parsley, chives and mint and a good seasoning of freshly milled pepper, then shake them over a very gentle heat so that each one gets a good coating of butter and herbs.

Lemon Parsley Potatoes

For two or three people:

1 chicken stock cube
1 lb potatoes
2 oz butter
2 teaspoons lemon juice
2 spring onions, finely chopped, including the green part
2 tablespoons finely chopped parsley
Salt and freshly milled black pepper

First, put $\frac{3}{4}$ pint water in a medium saucepan with the chicken stock cube crumbled into it, together with a little salt, and bring to the boil.

Meanwhile, peel and cut the potatoes into $\frac{1}{4}$-inch dice, add them to the simmering chicken stock and simmer very gently for 5 to 8 minutes – without a lid because you need to see what is happening – they need to be just tender and not mushy.

Now drain off the stock, return the potatoes to the pan and add the butter, lemon juice, spring onions and parsley, some freshly milled black pepper and a little more salt if it needs it. Swirl the potatoes round and round to get them all nice and buttery, and serve immediately.

Potatoes Niçoise

For two people:

1 small red or green pepper, chopped small
1 small onion, chopped small
1 clove garlic, crushed
1 lb cooked potatoes, roughly chopped
1 tablespoon fresh snipped chives (or fresh parsley)
2 tablespoons olive oil
2 tablespoons butter
Salt and freshly milled black pepper

In a large thick frying pan, melt half the butter and oil and gently cook the onion in it for 5 minutes, then add the garlic and chopped pepper and cook for a further 5 minutes. Now, using a slotted draining spoon, remove the onion, pepper and garlic and keep on one side.

Turn the heat up a bit and add the other half of the oil and butter to the pan. When it begins to sizzle, add the potatoes and fry them until they are crisp and golden on all sides.

When the potatoes are almost ready, replace the onions, pepper and garlic, stir them round a bit and allow to heat through. Then season with salt and freshly milled pepper, and sprinkle on the chives or parsley just before serving.

Potatoes Savoyard

For four people:

1½ lb potatoes	1 oz butter
1 small onion, finely chopped	3 oz grated Gruyère cheese
2 cloves garlic, crushed	Freshly milled black pepper
½ pint stock	Salt
1 tablespoon milk	

Pre-heat the oven to gas mark 5 (375°F).

I always use a meat roasting tin for this (although an ovenproof dish will do) and it should be very generously buttered. Peel and slice the potatoes (not too thinly, about ¼-inch thick). Arrange a layer of potatoes in the bottom of the tin, season with pepper and salt, then sprinkle on a little of the chopped onion, crushed garlic and grated cheese.

Continue in layers like this until everything is used up – finishing with a layer of potatoes. Pour in the stock and milk, cover with flecks of butter and bake uncovered in the oven for 45 minutes to 1 hour, until the potatoes are cooked and the top is a nice golden-brown.

To vary this a little you could add a scraping of nutmeg to the potato, or sprinkle a little crushed rosemary over the top.

Rosti

For four people:

2 lb potatoes
1 onion, very finely chopped
½ oz butter

Salt and freshly milled black pepper
Olive oil (about 2 to 3 tablespoons)

First, scrub the potatoes clean, then place them in a saucepan with enough boiling water to cover, and simmer until the potatoes are barely tender. Then, remove the pan from the heat, cover and leave for about 15 minutes, after which the potatoes should be drained and peeled. Now coarsely grate each potato into a bowl, add the onion and some small flakes of butter and season with salt and freshly milled black pepper. Toss the mixture with two forks to combine the ingredients very lightly, being careful not to crush the potato.

Next, heat the oil in a heavy frying pan, add the potato mixture and fry over a moderate heat, patting the mixture lightly into a neat cake shape. Cook for 10 to 15 minutes, by when the underside should be golden-brown (shake the pan occasionally during the cooking to prevent any sticking). Turn the rosti out on to a large warmed plate, then quickly return it to the pan to brown the other side. Serve cut into wedges.

Ratatouille Niçoise

To serve four:

2 large aubergines
2 medium onions
3 medium courgettes
4 large tomatoes (or a 14-oz tin Italian tomatoes, very well drained)
2 green (or red) peppers

2 cloves garlic, crushed to a pulp
1 level teaspoon dried basil
4 tablespoons olive oil
Salt and freshly milled black pepper

Badly made ratatouille can end up being rather mushy and not very attractive, so there are two points worth mentioning straight away: first, avoid cutting the vegetables too small (so that they can retain their shape and individuality); second, the aubergines and the courgettes must be drained at the start to get rid of excess moisture – which incidentally, is not half the bother it sounds.

So, to begin with, wipe the aubergines, cut them into 1-inch slices, then cut the slices in half. Similarly, wipe the courgettes and cut them into 1-inch slices. Now put the whole lot into a colander, sprinkle with plenty of salt, press them down with a plate and weigh the plate down (either with weights or a heavy object). Leave them like this for an hour or so, and this will also remove any bitterness from the aubergines.

Meanwhile, chop the onions coarsely and then do the same with the peppers, having de-seeded them and removed their cores. Skin the tomatoes by plunging them into boiling water for a minute or two, then peel and quarter them and remove the seeds.

Now, to start cooking the ratatouille, take a large saucepan and gently fry the chopped onions and crushed garlic in the oil for a good 10 minutes, then add the peppers. Meanwhile, dry the courgettes and aubergines in a clean cloth or some kitchen paper, then throw them in with the onions. Next, add the basil and some salt and freshly milled black pepper, have one really good stir, then simmer very gently (with the lid on) for 30 minutes. Finally, add the roughly chopped tomatoes, taste to check the seasoning, and cook for a further 15 minutes with the lid on.

Serve either on its own for lunch or as an accompaniment to a main meal. Ratatouille keeps well and does not mind being re-heated (gently), so it can be made well in advance.

Rice

Cooking rice needn't be a problem if a few simple rules are followed. The first rule is always buy good-quality long-grain rice; secondly, it is better to measure rice and liquid by volume rather than by weight; and most important of all, don't keep opening the cooking pot and giving it hefty stirs – because this will break the grains, release the starch and cause the rice to become soggy. Don't stir it at all during the cooking, just wait until all the liquid has been absorbed, then tip the rice into a serving dish and fluff it *gently* with a fork.

Boiled rice

For plain boiled rice for 4 people, use 1 large cup (or mug) of long-grain rice, place it in a saucepan with some salt, add 2½ times the same cup of boiling water, stir *once*, then put the lid on and let it simmer for 20 to 25 minutes until the grains are tender and the liquid has been absorbed.

Spiced Pilau Rice
To serve four:

1 teacup long-grain rice	1 heaped teaspoon ground turmeric
2½ teacups hot chicken stock (made with the giblets or with a cube)	4 cloves
	½ level teaspoon salt
2 oz butter	½ inch whole stick cinnamon
½ medium onion, finely chopped	Freshly milled black pepper

Begin by melting the butter in a thick-based saucepan and gently cook the onions in it for about 5 minutes, then add the rice and stir it around with a wooden spoon so that it gets a nice coating of butter. Now stir in the turmeric and pour in the hot chicken stock, then add the cloves, cinnamon and seasoning. Stir just once, and when it reaches boiling point put a lid on and simmer gently for 20 to 25 minutes, or until all the liquid is absorbed and the rice is tender.

When it's ready, take out the cinnamon and cloves (which will very conveniently have come to the top of the rice), empty the rice into a serving dish and fluff the grains with a fork to separate them.

Onion Rice
This is made exactly the same way as Spiced Pilau Rice, but omitting the spices.

Mashed Swedes with Bacon

For four to six people:

2 lb swedes
6 rashers bacon, chopped small
2 oz butter

2 tablespoons cream
Salt and freshly milled black
   pepper

First, peel the swedes and cut into smallish cubes; place them in a saucepan, then pour over enough water to just cover. Add salt and simmer for 20 to 30 minutes, or until the cubes are tender when tested with a skewer.

Pour the swedes into a colander to drain thoroughly and return the saucepan to the heat, adding a knob of butter and quickly frying the chopped bacon until it is just beginning to crisp.

Now return the swedes to the saucepan and mash to a creamy pulp, adding the rest of the butter and 2 tablespoons single cream. Season well with salt and freshly milled black pepper and serve piled on to a warm serving dish.

Spiced Stuffed Tomatoes

For four people:

8 large, firm and ripe tomatoes
½ teacupful Italian rice (or
   long-grain rice)
1 tablespoon pine nuts
   (available from healthfood
   shops, Greek shops and
   delicatessens)
1 tablespoon currants

1 small onion, chopped small
1½ teacups chicken stock
1 clove garlic, crushed
¼ teaspoon thyme
¼ teaspoon ground cinnamon
Olive oil
Pepper, salt and sugar

Pre-heat the oven to gas mark 4 (350°F).

Prepare the rice first by melting the onion and crushed garlic in oil over a low heat, then adding the rice, cinnamon, thyme, pine nuts and currants. Stir till the oil is completely absorbed, then add some salt and freshly milled black pepper.

Pour on the stock (it can be made with chicken stock cube), stir once, put on the lid and leave to simmer gently for 25 to 30 minutes until all the liquid has disappeared.

Give the pan a shake now and then to stop the rice sticking, but do not stir because the rice will break and become all sticky and starchy. In any case, if you use Italian rice it is not meant to be fluffy and separate – it is more puddingy than ordinary long-grain rice. When the rice is cooked, taste it to check the seasoning.

To prepare the tomatoes, slice off a little of the round end cleanly, then using a small sharp knife, scoop out all the seeds, leaving as much of the flesh behind as possible. Into each tomato put a pinch of sugar, then stuff them with the rice mixture and replace the lids. Put them into a meat roasting tin with a little water in the bottom, pour a little drop of olive oil over each one and bake them for 25 to 30 minutes. They can be eaten warm or cold, whichever you prefer.

Vegetable Curry

For two people:

½ lb potatoes, cut into smallish chunks
¼ lb carrots, sliced
1 celery stalk, sliced
1 medium onion, sliced
1 small cooking apple, peeled and chopped small
3 courgettes, sliced in ½-inch rounds
1 clove garlic, crushed
1 tablespoon flour
Curry powder
1 tablespoon tomato purée
½ oz chopped raisins
Juice of ½ lemon
Butter, cooking oil
Salt and freshly milled black pepper

Bring a medium saucepan of salted water to boiling point, then throw in the carrots and let them cook for 5 minutes; add the potatoes and let them cook for a further 8 minutes. Now drain (reserving the cooking water) and keep warm.

Heat about 1 tablespoon oil and ½ oz butter in a saucepan and gently fry the onions and garlic for 5 minutes, then add the celery, apple and courgettes and cook for a further 5 minutes, stirring everything round. Stir in the flour and 1 dessertspoon Madras curry powder (or more according to taste) and let that soak up the juices for a minute or two, then measure ½ pint of the vegetable water, stir the tomato purée into it, and add that to the saucepan a little at a time, stirring it in then adding the raisins.

Simmer very gently for about 10 minutes, stirring occasionally, then add the carrots and potatoes; cover, and cook for a further 15 minutes. Just before serving, season with salt, pepper and lemon juice.

Serve with rice and mango chutney.

SALADS

Raw Cauliflower and Mushroom Salad

For four people:

1 small cauliflower
¼ lb mushrooms
1 bunch spring onions
4 sticks celery

1 tablespoon fresh chopped
   parsley
2 heaped tablespoons fresh
   chopped mint

Remove the outer green, stalky leaves from the cauliflower, then trim off all the little florets and their tiny stalks, discarding the main stalk. Wash the cauliflower pieces, dry them in a clean cloth, then place them in a large salad bowl. The mushrooms should be washed and dried, then sliced very thinly through the stalks, and added to the cauliflower. Chop the celery and spring onions very small, add them to the salad bowl and mix well, finally adding the parsley and fresh chopped mint.

Just before serving, add a dressing made with:

1 teaspoon lemon juice
½ teaspoon sugar
A little dry mustard

Salt and freshly milled black
   pepper
5 or 6 teaspoons mild olive oil

Toss the salad very thoroughly in the dressing before serving.

New Potato Salad with Fresh Herbs

For four people:

2 lb new potatoes
8 medium-sized spring onions,
   very finely chopped
3 tablespoons fresh chopped
   mint
2 tablespoons fresh snipped
   chives
2 tablespoons fresh chopped
   parsley

for the dressing:

1 tablespoon wine vinegar
5 tablespoons olive oil
1 teaspoon dry mustard
1½ teaspoons salt
15 full turns freshly milled
   black pepper
1 clove garlic, crushed
1 dessertspoon fresh chopped
   tarragon (if available)

Make the dressing by letting the salt dissolve in the vinegar with the mustard, garlic and pepper for about 30 minutes, then add the tarragon and oil, and shake vigorously in a screw-top jar. Put the potatoes (whole but with the skins left on) in a saucepan with salt and a sprig or two of mint. Pour boiling water on them and cook for 20 to 25 minutes until cooked but still firm. Drain well, then put them in a salad bowl, roughly chop them with a sharp knife, then pour the dressing on while the potatoes are still warm (you may not need all the dressing). Add the fresh chopped herbs and spring onions, and mix well. This salad can, in fact, be made several hours in advance.

Rice Salad

For four people:

1 small teacup long-grain rice	2 tablespoons vinaigrette
2½ teacups boiling water	dressing
½ teaspoon salt	

Bring the water (salted) to the boil, add the rice and when the water comes back to the boil stir once and let it simmer with the lid on for 20 to 25 minutes until all the liquid is absorbed.

Empty the rice into a salad bowl and fluff it gently with a fork, and while the rice is still warm pour over 2 tablespoons vinaigrette dressing. When it is quite cold, add the following ingredients:

2 tablespoons fresh chopped parsley	½ red or green pepper, finely chopped
2 or 3 spring onions, finely chopped	2-inch piece cucumber, finely chopped
1 heaped tablespoon chopped walnuts	2 large tomatoes, peeled, de-seeded and finely chopped
1 heaped tablespoon currants	

Now mix the salad well, taste to check the seasoning, adding more salt and freshly milled pepper if necessary.

Wholefood Salad

For two people:

¼ medium white cabbage
3 new carrots
1 large red dessert apple
2 sticks celery, chopped small
2 oz walnuts, finely chopped
2 dessertspoons currants
4 spring onions, finely chopped
2 tablespoons fresh chopped parsley
1 tablespoon lemon juice

for the dressing:
1 clove garlic, crushed
1 level teaspoon salt
1 level teaspoon dry mustard
1 teaspoon wine vinegar
6 teaspoons olive oil
Salt and freshly milled black pepper

Make the dressing first, then prepare the cabbage by discarding the tough outer leaves and removing the stalk completely. Shred the cabbage quite finely using a sharp knife and put it into a large salad bowl. Add the carrots (which should be grated coarsely), then the chopped celery, spring onions, currants and nuts. The apple should be chopped quite small (with the skin left on) and tossed in lemon juice before being added to the rest of the ingredients. Now, mix everything together quite thoroughly, adding the fresh chopped parsley, then pour on the dressing and mix again thoroughly.

English Salad Sauce

For this you need:

Yolks of 3 hard-boiled eggs
¼ pint double cream
Salt

Cayenne pepper
4 teaspoons white wine vinegar (or tarragon vinegar)

Bring the eggs to the boil in plenty of cold water (they must be completely covered) and give them 8 minutes from when it starts boiling – must be timed properly to avoid them going black.

Run them under the cold tap to cool them down and stop them cooking any further. Peel off the shells and the whites, and put the yolks only into a mixing bowl. Add 1 tablespoon cold water

and pound them to a smooth paste with a wooden spoon; add a couple of pinches cayenne pepper and $\frac{1}{4}$ teaspoon salt, then gradually stir in the cream, bit by bit, mixing smoothly as you go.

When all the cream is in, add the vinegar and taste to check the seasoning. You may think you have gone wrong somewhere at this stage, because the mixture will appear to be far too runny. But fear not. Cover it and leave for a couple of hours in the refrigerator and it will miraculously have turned thicker (it should have the consistency of thickish cream rather than mayonnaise).

You can add a little garlic to the egg yolks or some anchovy sauce at the end. This, and a little tomato sauce to colour it, makes a lovely cocktail sauce for fresh prawns or crab. Or, if you can get hold of some fresh tarragon leaves and chop them into the sauce, it is excellent with cold salmon.

Mayonnaise

To make about $\frac{1}{2}$ pint (enough for four people) you need a basin approximately $1\frac{1}{2}$-pint size, a damp tea towel to put the basin on to keep it steady, and an electric mixer – the sort you hold in your hand – or a balloon whisk. The ingredients are:

2 large egg yolks	$\frac{1}{3}$ pint olive oil (in a small jug)
1 level teaspoon dry mustard	White wine vinegar (or
1 level teaspoon salt	tarragon vinegar, but *not*
A few screws black pepper	malt vinegar, which is far too
1 small clove garlic, crushed	strong)
(optional)	

Start off by mixing the egg yolks thoroughly with the salt, mustard and pepper; then, holding the jug in one hand and the whisk in the other, add just 1 drop of oil. When that has been whisked in, add another drop, then another, making sure each drop is thoroughly whisked in. In just a few minutes, after several drops, the mixture will start to thicken and then you can begin adding bigger drops, splodges even. Once it has thickened you know you are past danger-point.

When about half the oil is in, you can add 1 teaspoonful white wine vinegar; this will make the mixture thinner, and at this point you can start pouring in the oil in a steady continuous stream (whisking all the time) until it is all in. If you are not all-in by this time, taste it. Add more salt and pepper, if you think it needs it, and maybe a drop more vinegar.

Store the mayonnaise in a screw-top jar in a cool place. They say you should not keep it in the refrigerator, though I have no idea why; I have kept mayonnaise on the bottom shelf of the refrigerator for up to a week without any ill effects.

Note: If the mayonnaise curdles (and this will happen if the oil is added too quickly at the beginning), instead of throwing it out when no one is looking, simply separate another egg yolk into a clean bowl and then add the curdled mixture to it, drop by drop.

A lot of people prefer to use lemon juice rather than vinegar, and this is simply a matter of personal preference.

9 Puddings, Hot and Cold

If you were to ask me what contribution, now that we are members of the Common Market, this country could make to the Community's Cuisine, I would say that a pretty fair case could be made out for the Great British Pudding. You would think that it would have taken a really exotic dish to get a Frenchman hysterical with admiration for anyone else's cooking but his own, but read on: 'Blessed be he that invented pudding! For it is manna that hits the palates of all sorts of people, better even than that of the wilderness. Ah! what an excellent thing is an English pudding!'

How about that for a testimonial? It came from a Frenchman, Misson de Valbourg. True, that was at the end of the 17th century, but from then on we got even better at them. George I ('Pudding George') was particularly partial to his boiled pudding – hence the nursery-rhyme about Georgie Porgie – and by the time Queen Victoria had consented to give her royal approval to the pudding, this delicacy was being devoured all over the kingdom. It was quite common to see plum duffs and currant dumplings sold in the streets of London for a halfpenny each, while up at the Palace the royal chefs were creating yet more variations (which we still know well today), Queen's Pudding, Windsor Pudding, Empress Pudding, Albert Pudding.

If he had lived 150 years later, how much more ecstatically would that nice French tourist have written: 'To come at pudding time is to come at the most happy moment in the world!'

Apple and Almond Pudding

For four to six people:

1 lb cooking apples
2 oz soft brown sugar
4 oz ground almonds

4 oz butter (at room temperature)
4 oz caster sugar
2 eggs, beaten

Cut up the apples and stew till soft with the brown sugar and approximately 1 tablespoon water, then arrange them in the bottom of a buttered pie dish. In a mixing bowl, cream the butter and sugar until pale, light and fluffy, then beat in the eggs a little at a time, and when they are all in fold in the ground almonds. Spread this mixture over the apples, making the surface even with the back of a spoon, and bake in a pre-heated oven (gas mark 4, 350°F), for exactly 1 hour.

This pudding can be served warm or cold, and will keep in the refrigerator for up to a week. But either way it is nice served with a dollop of thick cream.

Apple Cream Flan

To serve six people:

4 large cooking apples
2 oz butter
2 level tablespoons caster sugar
3 wheatmeal biscuits, crushed into crumbs
¼ whole nutmeg, grated

2 tablespoons brandy
Grated peel of 1 small lemon
⅛ pint double cream
3 egg yolks
6 oz shortcrust pastry (made, with 4 oz plain flour, 2 oz fat)

Pre-heat the oven to gas mark 4 (350°F). For this recipe you will need an 8-inch flan tin, lightly greased.

First, roll out the pastry and line the flan tin. Prick the base all over with a fork, and bake it for about 20 minutes. Peel, core and slice the apples, then put them in a saucepan with a couple of tablespoons water and cook quickly until they are soft. Now drain, and empty them into a large mixing bowl and beat them to a pulp (the best thing for this is an electric hand-whisk).

While the apple pulp is still hot, beat in 2 oz butter and enough sugar to sweeten it to your taste (you may not need 2 heaped tablespoons). Stir in the grated lemon peel, the biscuit crumbs, nutmeg and brandy. Mix very thoroughly and leave it to cool.

Meanwhile, you can be whisking the egg yolks and lightly whipping the cream to thicken it very slightly (but not too much). Now, stir the egg yolks into the cooled apple mixture, then the cream, and then turn the whole lot into the half-cooked pastry-case and bake it (at the same temperature) for about 30 minutes. Serve it warm if you like, but it is equally good chilled.

Apple Nut Crumble

For four to six people:

2 lb cooking apples	*for the topping:*
3 oz sultanas	3 oz butter
4 oz soft dark brown sugar	6 oz wholemeal flour
¼ teaspoon powdered cloves	3 oz brown sugar
1 teaspoon ground cinnamon	3 oz chopped nuts
1 dessertspoon lemon juice	

Pre-heat the oven to gas mark 4 (350°F), with a baking sheet.

Peel, core and slice the apples thinly, then in a bowl mix the apples, sultanas, sugar and spices and sprinkle with lemon juice. Now pack the mixture into a well-buttered baking dish.

To make the crumble topping, rub the butter into the flour and sugar until the mixture resembles fine breadcrumbs. Stir in the chopped nuts, then sprinkle the mixture over the top of the apples.

Place the dish on the baking sheet in the centre of the oven, and cook for about 1 hour, or until the apple slices are tender and the top is crisp and golden.

Serve with custard or cream.

Brown Apple Pudding

To serve four to six people:

14 slices brown bread, cut from a small loaf
4 oz (approx.) softened butter
1½ lb cooking apples

Rind and juice of 1 large lemon
3 oz soft light brown sugar
1 oz sultanas
½ teaspoon mixed spice

Butter the bread slices generously and remove the crusts. Then butter a 2-pint pudding basin, lining the base and sides of it with some of the bread slices (buttered sides facing inwards). Peel and core the apples, cut them into small chunks and toss them with the lemon rind and juice, the sugar, sultanas and spice. Now pack half the apple mixture into the bread-lined basin and dot the surface with a few flecks of butter.

Then cover the surface with more bread slices (buttered side up) and fill to the top with the remaining apple mixture. Press lightly, dot with more flecks of butter, and finally cover the surface with the rest of the slices (buttered side down).

Cover the basin tightly with a sheet of greaseproof paper, then with a sheet of foil, and secure with string. Steam the pudding for 1½ hours.

Serve with cream or a rich custard sauce.

Fresh Apricot and Almond Tart

For six people:

6 oz wholemeal self-raising flour
3 oz butter or margarine
1 large egg
2 level tablespoons soft brown sugar

1½ lb fresh apricots, stoned and halved
1 level teaspoon ground cinnamon
1 oz flaked almonds
A little extra sugar

Pre-heat the oven to gas mark 4 (350°F). You will need an oblong baking tin, 11 × 7 in., buttered.

Sift the flour into a large mixing bowl, then rub in the butter with your fingertips. When it is nice and crumbly, mix in the sugar, then make a well in the centre, break the egg into it and start to mix it in with a large fork. Finish off with your hands to make a smooth dough. If the mixture seems a little dry, add a tiny spot of milk. Transfer the pastry on to the baking tin, press it out all over the base with your hands (flour them if they get a bit sticky). Arrange the apricot halves all over the pastry, sprinkle the cinnamon and almonds all over, with just a little more sugar, then bake for 45 minutes. Serve warm with cream.

Brown Bread Pudding with Brandy Butter

To serve six:

½ lb stale brown breadcrumbs	Grated zest of a smallish
½ lb shredded suet	lemon
½ lb prepared currants	½ teaspoon salt
3 oz soft dark, brown sugar	½ nutmeg, freshly grated
2 oz whole candied orange and	5 eggs
lemon peel, finely chopped	4 tablespoons brandy

To make this lovely aromatic pudding you will need a ½-pint pudding basin; serve it hot with icy cold brandy butter to melt over it.

Begin by putting the breadcrumbs into a large mixing bowl, followed by the shredded suet, currants and soft brown sugar. Mix all these together thoroughly. Now add the candied peel, chopped small, the grated zest of the lemon, salt and grated nutmeg, then mix again thoroughly.

Finally, add the eggs (which should be well-beaten) and the brandy. Now, using a wooden spoon, stir for not less than 5 minutes to get everything well and truly mixed together (I cannot emphasize the stirring too much). Butter the pudding basin generously, then pack the mixture into it, tie the pudding with greaseproof paper and foil, and steam for 3½ hours.

Brandy Butter

3 oz unsalted butter	2½ tablespoons brandy
3 oz caster sugar	1 teaspoon lemon juice

Have the butter at room temperature before you begin, then beat with a wooden spoon until it becomes very white and creamy.

Now, add the sugar a little at a time, beating well after each addition. When all the sugar is in, start adding the brandy a few drops at a time, still beating. Finally, beat in the lemon juice, transfer the butter to a serving dish, and chill for 2 to 3 hours.

Moist Chocolate Pudding

To serve three or four:

2 oz plain chocolate, roughly chopped	2 large eggs, separated
$\frac{1}{4}$ pint single cream	$1\frac{1}{2}$ oz stale white breadcrumbs
2 teaspoons instant coffee (granules or powder)	1 teaspoon butter
	1 or 2 drops vanilla essence

Pre-heat the oven to gas mark 4 (350°F).

Begin by buttering, generously, a $1\frac{1}{2}$-pint baking dish, and placing a basin over a pan of barely simmering water. Melt the butter in the basin, then add the chocolate, cream and coffee. Stir till everything is melted and thoroughly amalgamated.

In another basin, whisk the egg yolks, then pour in the chocolate mixture (whisking all the time), stir in the breadcrumbs and allow the mixture to cool. Then stir in the vanilla essence and, after whisking the egg whites till stiff, carefully fold them into the chocolate and breadcrumb mixture. Pour the whole lot into the baking dish, and bake in the oven until the pudding is well risen, has stopped making bubbling noises and feels firm in the centre (45 to 60 minutes).

Serve immediately, with either pouring cream or hot chocolate sauce. The sauce can be made by putting 4 oz plain chocolate in a basin with 2 tablespoons water and a small knob of butter, then sitting the basin in a pan of barely simmering water.)

Crêpes Suzette

To serve four to six people:

For the batter:

4 oz plain flour	2 tablespoons melted unsalted
A pinch of salt	butter (approx. 1 oz)
2 large fresh eggs	1 level tablespoon caster sugar
7 fl. oz milk and 3 fl. oz water, mixed together	Grated rind of an orange

I have always felt that the frequently heard recommendation about leaving batter to stand before being used was just culinary jiggery-pokery, and have demonstrated that waiting makes no difference in the final result.

To make the batter, sieve the flour and salt into a largish mixing bowl, then make a well in the centre and break 2 eggs into it. Now start to whisk the eggs, incorporating bits of flour from the edges. Add a drop of milk-and-water from time to time and ignore the lumps – they will disappear later.

When all the milk has been slowly added to the eggs and flour, give everything a thorough whisking (with a hand-held electric mixer, or a rotary or balloon whisk).

When the batter is frothy and bubbly and all the lumps have vanished, it is ready; it should be the consistency of thin cream. At this stage whisk in 1 tablespoon caster sugar and the finely grated orange rind. Finally, just before you are ready to cook the crêpes, add 2 tablespoons melted butter, and pour the batter into a jug.

To make perfect crêpes, you need a small, very heavy frying pan with an inside base of not more than 7 inches in diameter (if your pan is any larger, you will have a hard time getting your crêpes thin enough without going all ragged round the edges). Start by putting 1 teaspoon butter in the pan, melt it, swirl it round and round to lubricate the pan thoroughly (not forgetting the sides), then empty any excess butter on to a saucer.

Now get your pan fairly hot. It's impossible to be exact, but I have found that once the pan itself was really hot, a medium heat underneath was about right. The first crêpe can be a practice one, to test the right amount of batter needed – about 1 tablespoonful plus 1 almost full tablespoon. As soon as the batter reaches the hot pan, tip it round from side to side so that it covers the base completely.

Crêpes should be so thin that they cook through in a few seconds: there is no need to toss or turn them over – as soon as the upper side stops looking runny, it is cooked. All you do then is carefully lift it from the pan with a palette knife and transfer it to a plate, then get on with the next one.

You should not find it necessary to add any more butter till about half-way through, and you should get 16 to 18 crêpes all told. They can be stacked on top of each other on a plate and, if you are serving them to guests, the crêpes can be made several hours beforehand.

For the sauce:

5 fl. oz freshly squeezed orange juice (from 3 or 4 medium oranges)
Grated rind of 1 medium orange
Juice of 1 small lemon
Grated rind of 1 small lemon

1 level tablespoon caster sugar
3 tablespoons Orange Curaçao, Grand Marnier, Cointreau or Brandy (you get 3 tablespoons from a miniature bottle)
2 oz unsalted butter

Mix all the ingredients except the butter, and warm the plates on which the crêpes are to be served. Now, take the largest frying pan you have (9½–10 inches would be ideal). Melt 2 oz butter in it, then add the rest of the ingredients and allow the mixture to heat through very gently.

Now, pop in your first crêpe, let it heat through, fold it in half and then in half again (to a triangular shape), move it to the edge of the pan and pop the next one in. Continue like this until all the crêpes are folded and well impregnated with the sauce.

Perhaps a modest tablespoon of flames may not add much to the flavour, but it could add a lot to your prestige as a cook, so heat a tablespoon directly over the gas flame or resting on an electric hotplate. Pour brandy or liqueur into it, warm that, then set light to it. Carry it to the table along with the frying pan and pour the flames over the crêpes just before serving.

Date and Walnut Pudding

For four to six people:

3 oz self-raising flour
3 oz fresh white breadcrumbs
3 oz suet (from a packet)
1½ oz soft light brown sugar
½ teaspoon ground ginger
½ teaspoon salt

4 oz pitted dates, chopped
2 oz walnuts, coarsely chopped
1 egg
Butter
4–6 tablespoons milk

Start by buttering a 1½-pint pudding basin generously, then put the flour, breadcrumbs, suet, sugar, ground ginger, salt, chopped dates and walnuts into a bowl. Next, beat the egg and milk together and then mix them into the dry ingredients very thoroughly – the mixture should be a nice soft dripping consistency that drops easily from the spoon.

Now, turn the mixture into the buttered basin and cover it tightly with a buttered sheet of greaseproof paper and a sheet of foil (pleated across the centre to allow the pudding room to expand); tie it securely with string, put the pudding in a steamer and steam for 2 hours.

To serve, remove the covering and turn the pudding out on to a warmed serving plate.

Frangipane Tart

For four to six people:

5 oz puff pastry (can be
    bought)
4 oz softened butter
4 oz caster sugar
2 standard eggs, beaten

4 oz ground almonds
1 oz plain flour
Almond essence
Vanilla essence
4 tablespoons raspberry jam

Pre-heat the oven, with a baking sheet inside, to gas mark 6 (400°F).

Line an 8 or 8½-inch (greased) flan tin with the thinly rolled-out puff pastry, and prick the base all over with a fork.

To make the filling, cream the butter and sugar till pale and fluffy, then add the beaten eggs, a little at a time, beating vigorously after each addition. Now, using a metal spoon, fold in the sifted flour and the ground almonds.

Add a few drops of almond essence and a few drops of vanilla essence, then stir to mix everything evenly. Spread the jam over the base of the pastry, then cover with the frangipane mixture, spreading evenly and bringing it right up to the edge of the pastry all round.

Place the tart on the pre-heated baking sheet and bake for 40 minutes, till well risen and golden-brown.

Lancaster Lemon Tart

Ingredients for six people:

3 rounded tablespoons lemon curd
3 oz butter (at room temperature)
4 oz self-raising flour
3 oz caster sugar
1 egg, beaten lightly

1 oz ground almonds
Grated rind and juice of a lemon
1½ oz whole almonds, peeled and halved
4 oz shortcrust pastry

Pre-heat the oven to gas mark 6 (400°F).

Line a 7-inch or 8-inch enamel pie-plate with pastry and spread the base with lemon curd. Now cream the butter and sugar together till light, pale and fluffy. Next, gradually beat in the egg, a teaspoonful at a time, then carefully fold in the ground almonds and flour, followed by the lemon rind and juice.

Spread the mixture over the lemon curd and smooth with a palette knife. Sprinkle the halved almonds on the surface, bake in the centre of the oven for 15 minutes, then reduce the heat to gas mark 2 (300°F), and continue cooking for a further 25 to 30 minutes.

Serve either warm or cold, with cream.

Lemon Meringue Pie

For four people:

4 oz shortcrust pastry	1 small lemon
1 packet lemon pie filling	3 eggs
½ pint water	6 oz caster sugar

Start by rolling out the pastry, then line a greased 8-inch round flan tin (or Pyrex pie dish) with it. Prick the bottom all over with a fork and bake it for about 30 minutes at gas mark 4 (350°F).

For the filling, separate the eggs, beat the yolks, and put them in a saucepan, together with the pie filling, the juice and grated rind of the lemon and ½ pint water.

Now bring to the boil, whisking with a balloon whisk to prevent lumps, and let it boil for a minute or two until thick.

Now whisk the whites till they form peaks, and gradually beat in the sugar, a tablespoonful at a time. Pour the lemon filling into the pastry case, then top with the meringue mixture, making sure it covers all the filling, and seal it in round the edges. Bake in a slow oven at gas mark 2 (300°F) for 30 minutes.

Traditional Lemon Pancakes

For four people:

4 oz plain flour	2 tablespoons melted butter
A pinch of salt	Lard
2 eggs	4 large lemons
1 fl. oz milk and 3 fl. oz water, mixed together	Caster sugar

For these you need a 7- or 8-inch heavy frying pan.

Sift the flour and salt into a bowl, make a well in the centre and break the eggs into it. Whisk the eggs, incorporating a little of the flour as you go, and when the mixture starts to get too thick, start adding the milk-and-water bit by bit, still whisking until it is all in and you have a smooth batter with the consistency of thin cream.

Just before you start to cook the pancakes, add the 2 table-spoons melted butter.

Have ready two plates in a warm oven, and pop the lemons in too (they squeeze more easily if warmed a bit). Melt a little lard in the pan, swirl it round to get the pan lubricated, and pour out any excess fat on to a saucer. When the pan is smoking hot, pour in 2 tablespoons batter, then turn the heat down to medium. Tip the pan from side to side so that the batter covers the base completely and when it is brown on the underside, flip it over, with or without the aid of a palette knife, and brown the other side. Then keep it warm between two plates in the oven while making the rest.

Serve with lemon juice squeezed and sugar sprinkled over, then roll up – and have extra lemon quarters and more sugar on the table.

Profiteroles in Hot Chocolate Sauce

For four people:

2½ oz plain flour
2 oz butter, diced
1 level teaspoon sugar
2 large eggs, well beaten
½ pint double cream, whipped
    thick

for the sauce:
½ lb plain chocolate and 3 tablespoons water (melted together in a basin either in the oven or over simmering water)

Pre-heat the oven to gas mark 7 (425°F), and grease a large baking tray.

Place the butter, 1 teaspoon sugar and ¼ pint cold water in a saucepan and bring to the boil. Sieve the flour on to a piece of paper and tip it into the saucepan all at once. Now remove the saucepan from the heat and beat vigorously until the paste is smooth and leaves the sides of the pan. Next, gradually beat in the egg mixture bit by bit, and at the end beat again until the mixture is smooth and glossy.

Now, place teaspoonfuls of the mixture on the baking tray and bake for 10 minutes – then reduce the heat to gas mark 3 (325°F) and bake for a further 15 to 20 minutes until the choux buns are crisp, light and a rich golden colour.

Cool on a wire rack, then just before serving split each one in half, fill with a teaspoonful of whipped cream and join the halves together again (don't be tempted to put the cream in ahead of time, because this tends to make them soggy). Pour the melted chocolate over them and serve immediately.

Queen of Puddings

For four people:

1 pint milk	Grated rind of a small lemon
4 oz fresh white breadcrumbs	2 eggs, separated
¼ oz butter	3 level tablespoons raspberry
2 oz caster sugar	jam

Start by buttering a 1½-pint oval pie dish rather generously and pre-heat the oven to gas mark 4 (350°F).

Bring the milk to the boil in a saucepan, then take it off the heat and stir in the butter, breadcrumbs, 1 oz sugar and the lemon rind, then leave it for 20 minutes (to allow the breadcrumbs to swell a bit). Separate the eggs, beat the yolks on their own and then into the cooled breadcrumb mixture. Now pour it into the pie dish, spread the surface evenly, then bake in the centre of the oven for 30 to 35 minutes, or until set.

Meanwhile, melt the jam in a saucepan over a low heat, then take the dish out of the oven and carefully spread the melted jam on to the top of the pudding. Whisk the egg whites until they are stiff, then whisk in 1 oz caster sugar, spoon the egg-white mixture all over the pudding, sprinkle 1 teaspoon caster sugar over and bake for another 10 to 15 minutes, until the meringue topping is golden-brown on top.

Raisin Pudding with Port Wine Sauce

To serve four people:

2 oz brown breadcrumbs	⅛ teaspoon ground mace
2 oz self-raising flour	1 oz whole candied peel, finely
6 oz shredded suet	chopped
½ lb prepared stoned raisins	Grated zest of 1 orange
⅛ teaspoon salt	3 eggs, well beaten
½ nutmeg, grated	3 tablespoons brandy
½ teaspoon ground ginger	

Put the breadcrumbs, flour and suet in a large mixing bowl, then add the raisins, making sure that you separate any that are stuck together (if you have bought them ready-stoned). Mix everything thoroughly and evenly, then add salt, nutmeg, mace, ginger, candied orange peel and orange zest. Mix it all again thoroughly.

Now add the beaten eggs and the brandy, then stir for at least 5 minutes to blend everything evenly. Pack the mixture into a well-buttered 1½-pint pudding basin, cover and tie with grease-proof paper and foil, and steam for 4 hours. To turn the pudding out, loosen it all round the sides with a palette knife, and turn on to a heated plate.

Port Wine Sauce

5 fl. oz ruby or tawny port	½ nutmeg, freshly grated
Grated zest of 1 Seville orange	1 tablespoon Seville orange
(an ordinary orange will do)	juice
2 oz caster sugar	1 oz unsalted butter
5 fl. oz water	1 teaspoon flour

Place the orange zest, water and sugar into a thick-bottomed saucepan and boil very gently together for 15 minutes. Mix the butter into the flour, then divide it up into about six pieces and add them to the syrup, followed by the port, nutmeg and orange juice. Keep stirring over a gentle flame and boil the mixture for one minute, then serve immediately.

(If you want to, you can prepare this sauce in advance, except for the butter and flour part, which should be added just before serving.)

Rhubarb and Ginger Tart

For this double-crust pie I use a 10-inch diameter enamelled plate, to serve four to six people:

Shortcrust pastry (made with 10 oz flour, a pinch of salt, 3 oz margarine and 3 oz lard)
2½ lb rhubarb, washed and cut into chunks
4 oz soft dark brown sugar
1 heaped teaspoon powdered ginger
A little milk
Caster sugar

Put the rhubarb in a saucepan, together with the sugar and ginger – without adding any water – and let it cook over a low heat till soft (remember to stir it round now and then). Now pour it into a large sieve and let it drain for about 10 minutes.

Grease the pie plate and line it with half the pastry, fill with rhubarb, cover with the remaining pastry. Make a few slits in the centre, brush with milk and bake in a pre-heated oven gas mark 5 (375° F) for about 40 minutes.

Dust with caster sugar and serve warm with thick cream.

Chocolate Orange Soufflé

For four people you need:

4 oz plain chocolate
Juice of a largish Seville orange or 2 tablespoons rum
4 egg yolks
6 egg whites (large eggs)
½ pint double cream
Icing sugar

Pre-heat the oven and a baking sheet to gas mark 6 (400° F). You will need a 2-pint soufflé dish, well buttered.

Break the chocolate into a mixing bowl, add the orange juice and put the bowl in the bottom of the oven for 5 to 10 minutes until the chocolate is soft.

Remove, then beat with a wooden spoon until it is smooth. Now whisk the egg yolks thoroughly and stir them into the chocolate.

Next, using a clean, dry whisk, beat the egg whites till stiff, fold them carefully into the chocolate mixture and pour the lot into the soufflé dish.

Place the dish on the baking sheet in the oven, then leave it for approximately 20 minutes, or until the soufflé is puffy and spongy to touch.

Dust the top with sieved icing sugar and serve immediately with the double cream in a jug to pour over separately (it is much better to serve running cream with this, rather than whipped cream).

Lemon Soufflé Omelette

To serve two people:

3 large eggs, separated	2 dessertspoons caster sugar
Juice and grated rind of 1 lemon	Butter

First add the grated rind and the juice of the lemon to the egg yolks, together with the sugar, and whisk until the mixture is slightly thick and creamy. Now start to melt the butter in a thick-based frying pan and turn the heat on the grill to its highest. Whisk the egg whites until stiff, then using a metal spoon carefully fold them into the yolks, lightly and quickly.

Now pour the lot on to the heated butter, then fold and stir a bit to prevent anything sticking to the bottom. After about 10 seconds place the pan under the grill, so that the top can brown nicely. Serve immediately straight from the pan.

For a special occasion you can warm a tablespoon, pour brandy into it, set light to the brandy, then carry your omelette to the table, pouring the lighted brandy over just before you get there.

Lemon Sponge Pudding

Ingredients for two servings:

4 oz caster sugar	¼ pint milk
2 oz butter	2 eggs, separated
Grated rind and juice of 2 lemons	2 oz plain flour
	A pinch of salt

Pre-heat the oven to gas mark 4 (350°F).

Begin by buttering a 1½-pint pie dish. Then cream 2 oz butter together with the sugar and grated lemon rind until the mixture is fluffy. Beat in the egg yolks, then gradually fold in the flour and salt, alternating with the milk. Now stir in the lemon juice.

In a separate basin beat the egg whites to a stiff consistency and fold them into the lemon mixture, which should then be poured into the pie dish. Place the dish in a small roasting tin and pour enough water into the tin to come half-way up the side of the pie dish. Bake until the top is golden and has risen well (about 50 to 60 minutes). Sprinkle a little caster sugar on top and serve immediately.

Treacle Sponge Pudding

For four people:

4 oz butter	1½ teaspoons ground ginger
4 oz caster sugar	1 tablespoon milk
2 eggs, beaten	Golden syrup
6 oz self-raising flour	

First butter a 1½-pint pudding basin, then in another bowl cream the butter and sugar together until light and fluffy. Next, beat in the eggs a little at a time, beating well between each addition. Then carefully fold in the sieved flour and ginger with a metal spoon, followed by the milk. Spoon 2 tablespoons golden syrup into the base of the buttered pudding basin, then spoon in the sponge mixture.

Cover the top of the basin with a sheet of buttered greaseproof paper (buttered side down), pleated once in the centre, and cover this with a sheet of foil pleated in the same way, then secure firmly with string. Place the pudding in a steamer over a saucepan of boiling water. Cover and steam the pudding for 2 hours, making sure that the water is kept on the boil throughout, and checking if the water level needs topping up at all.

Serve with extra warmed syrup poured over, or with custard.

Zabaglione

To make the authentic version you will need to have some genuine Marsala wine; this is widely available and is no more expensive than sherry. The ingredients for four people are:

8 egg yolks	4 dessertspoons caster sugar
3 fl. oz Marsala	

First find a mixing bowl or basin that will sit comfortably over a saucepan of boiling water. Into the basin put the egg yolks and sugar and whisk until the mixture is pale and creamy. Then gradually whisk in the Marsala, put the basin over a saucepan of just-simmering water, and continue whisking until the mixture thickens.

This operation does need a fair amount of patience as the mixture is usually slow to thicken (but do not raise the heat because if the mixture gets too hot or reaches boiling point, it is liable to curdle). When it has thickened, pour into 4 warmed wine glasses and serve immediately with plain *langues de chat* biscuits.

COLD PUDDINGS

Danish Apple Cake

For six to eight people:

2½ lb cooking apples, peeled, cored and sliced	8 oz dry white breadcrumbs
6 oz butter	3 tablespoons granulated sugar
4 oz soft brown sugar	1 tablespoon ground cinnamon
	2 teaspoons mixed spice

First, melt 2 oz butter in a medium-sized saucepan. Toss the sliced apples in the melted butter, then cover the saucepan with a well-fitting lid and cook very slowly until the apples are soft, shaking the pan from time to time to prevent them sticking. Beat in the brown sugar – taste, and add more brown sugar if it needs it – cover and leave until cool. Meanwhile, melt the remaining butter in a large frying pan and mix in the dried breadcrumbs, granulated sugar and spices. Stir thoroughly until well mixed. Now heat gently and continue stirring constantly until the mixture is an even, deep golden-brown, then remove the pan from the heat and leave to cool. Spread a quarter of the breadcrumbs in a pint-sized deep, round serving dish, and top with one-third of the apple pulp. Repeat this layering twice more, then sprinkle with the remaining breadcrumbs, and chill thoroughly.

Serve with whipped cream, sweetened and flavoured with vanilla.

Braziliar Bananas

For four people:

6 ripe bananas	2 teaspoons instant coffee
2 level tablespoons dark soft brown sugar	1 teaspoon boiling water
2 tablespoons rum (only if you have some handy)	½ pint double cream

First, put 2 teaspoons instant coffee in a cup with a teaspoon of boiling water to dissolve the coffee, then let it cool. Whip the cream till it is thick but not too stiff, and put half of it into another bowl for later. Add the dissolved coffee to the remaining cream, together with 1 tablespoon rum.

Now peel and slice the bananas and arrange them in a bowl. Sprinkle them with the other tablespoon of rum and 2 tablespoons brown sugar. Mix them around a bit, then add the coffee-flavoured cream and mix again. Spread a layer of plain whipped cream over the top, cover and chill if time permits.

(Should you happen to have a couple of tablespoons of strong Brazilian coffee already made, you could use that instead of the instant.)

Mrs Simpson's Cheesecake

This recipe will serve eight people, or would probably last four people a whole weekend.

½ lb wheatmeal biscuits	3 standard eggs
¼ lb butter	1 teaspoon vanilla essence
1½ lb curd cheese	½ pint double cream
½ lb sugar	Fruit (whatever is available)

You will require a 9-inch cake tin about 2–3 inches deep (a spring form tin would be ideal). Pre-heat the oven to gas mark 2 (300°F).

Gently melt the butter in a small saucepan without letting it brown, crush the biscuits to fine crumbs with a rolling pin, then stir them in the melted butter. Transfer the biscuit mixture into the cake tin and press it down evenly all over to form a base. The curd cheese, eggs and sugar should be mixed together to form a smooth, thick cream (an electric mixer is best for this), then mix in the vanilla essence and pour the mixture over the biscuit base, and smooth it out evenly. Cook the cheesecake for 30 minutes, then turn the oven off and leave the cheesecake to get quite cold in the oven. It should then be chilled for at least 2 hours, or preferably overnight.

To serve the cake, top it with whipped cream and fruit – fresh raspberries are especially good, but failing them, well-drained pineapple is also delicious.

Cold Chocolate Orange Soufflé

For four people:

7 oz plain chocolate
3 eggs, whole
2 eggs, separated
3 oz caster sugar
Grated rind and juice of
  1 orange

2 fl. oz water
½ oz powdered gelatine
3 fl. oz double cream, lightly
  whipped

Soak the powdered gelatine in the orange juice in an old cup, then stand it in a pan of barely simmering water until it has dissolved and is quite transparent.

Meanwhile place the 2 egg yolks, 3 whole eggs and sugar in a basin fitted over a pan of simmering water, and whisk with an electric mixer until the mixture is thick and creamy.

Remove the basin from the heat, then put another basin, containing the broken-up chocolate and water, over the simmering water.

When the chocolate has melted, stir till smooth, add the grated orange rind and, when it has cooled, stir it into the egg mixture.

Now pour the melted gelatine through a strainer into the mixture, mix thoroughly and, when the mixture is just at the point of setting, carefully fold in the lightly whipped cream and the stiffly beaten egg whites.

Pour the mixture into a soufflé dish, cover and chill until set. Decorate with some more whipped double cream, a few orange segments and a little grated chocolate.

Coeur à la Crème

For four people:

8 oz unsalted cream cheese
½ pint soured cream
2 level tablespoons caster sugar

2 large egg whites
4 tablespoons double cream

In a mixing bowl thoroughly combine the cream cheese, soured cream and sugar. Then whisk the egg whites till stiff and fold them carefully into the mixture. Now place the mixture in a suitably sized piece of muslin (or fine gauze) and put it in a sieve over a bowl to drain thoroughly overnight in a cool place.

Serve it piled into individual dishes, with either fresh raspberries or fresh strawberries piled on top and the double cream poured over.

Damson Cream

For six people:

2 lb damsons	¾ pint double cream, lightly
6 oz caster sugar	whipped
3 egg whites	

Put the damsons in a large saucepan with ¼ pint water and 6 oz sugar. Bring to the boil and cook gently (without a lid) for about 10 minutes or until the damsons are soft and pulpy.

Now take a large sieve, place it over a large bowl and pour the contents of the saucepan into the sieve, and leave until all the excess liquid has drained away. Keep the syrup in the bowl on one side, then place the sieve over another bowl and rub the damsons through (extracting all the stones). When the mixture is quite cold, carefully fold the lightly whipped cream into the damson purée. Now, whisk the egg whites till stiff, and carefully fold them also into the mixture. Pour this mixture into 6 individual stemmed glasses, cover and chill for at least 3 or 4 hours. Just before serving, spoon the remaining damson syrup over each portion.

Fresh Lemon Gateau

For six people:

1 packet trifle sponges	4 eggs, separated
(8 sponges)	2 large lemons
4 oz unsalted butter	½ pint double cream
6 oz caster sugar	

For this I recommend using a 2-pint earthenware casserole, but a 2-pint pudding basin will do.

In a large mixing bowl, cream the butter and sugar till very pale and fluffy, then whisk the egg yolks and beat them into the butter and sugar mixture, a teaspoonful at a time, beating well after each addition. (An electric whisk is best for this operation.)

Now, add the grated rinds of both lemons and their juice, beating in a little at a time. Next, whisk the egg whites till they form soft peaks, then using a metal spoon fold them into the mixture. Don't worry about the mixture curdling at this point, because for once it doesn't matter.

Split the sponge cakes in half lengthways, then place a layer of them in the base of the bowl followed by a layer of the curdled mixture – and so on, finishing off with a layer of sponge. Now cover with foil and put a plate on top, then refrigerate overnight.

To serve, turn out, cut into slices and serve with pouring cream. Alternatively, when the cake is turned out you could cover it with whipped cream and decorate with crystallized lemon slices.

Coffee and Walnut Mousse

For three to four people:

2 egg yolks
2–3 dessertspoons strong. instant coffee (made with 1 dessertspoon coffee and 2 dessertspoons boiling water)
1 oz chopped walnuts

¼ pint thick cream
¼ oz powdered gelatine
⅛ pint water
3 egg whites
4 dessertspoons caster sugar

Place the gelatine and water in a small basin fitted over a pan of hot (not boiling) water. When the gelatine has dissolved completely it will be absolutely transparent. Whisk the egg yolks, sugar and coffee in a bowl over another pan of hot water until they are thick and creamy, then remove from the heat and continue to whisk until cool.

Add the chopped walnuts to the mixture and strain the dissolved gelatine into it, mix thoroughly, now place it in a cool place to set and when it is on the point of setting, whisk the cream lightly and fold it in gently, alternating with the stiffly beaten egg whites.

Pour the mixture into a serving dish and chill till set. Before serving, decorate the top with approximately ⅛ pint whipped cream, and a few extra walnuts if you feel like it.

Fresh Lemon Mousse

For four people:

3 large eggs, separated   ½ oz powdered gelatine
4 oz caster sugar   ¼ pint double cream
3 small (or 2 large) lemons   2 fl. oz. hot water

First, separate the eggs and put the yolks, sugar and the grated rind and juice of the lemons into a basin. Stand the basin over a saucepan of gently simmering water, and whisk with a rotary whisk for about 6 minutes until the mixture thickens. Then, remove the basin from the heat and continue whisking for a few more minutes until it is pale and creamy, and has cooled off a bit.

Now, dissolve the gelatine in a cold cup with 2 fl. oz hot water – stand the cup in the pan of simmering water you used before, and leave it like that until the gelatine is completely dissolved and has turned transparent.

Next, add the dissolved gelatine to the egg-yolk mixture, lightly whip the cream until it just begins to thicken, then fold half of it into the egg-yolk mixture.

Finally, beat the egg whites until stiff, then, using a metal spoon, lightly fold them into the rest of the mixture. Turn the mixture into a suitably sized serving dish. Cover and chill for several hours.

Serve with the rest of the lightly whipped cream in the bowl to spoon on top.

Pavlova with Peaches

For six people:

3 large fresh egg whites   ½ pint double cream
6 oz caster sugar   4 firm, ripe medium peaches,
1 level teaspoon cornflour   peeled and sliced
½ teaspoon vinegar   Icing sugar

Pre-heat the oven to gas mark 2 (300°F).

Prepare a baking sheet by oiling it and lining it with greaseproof paper (and oiling that slightly). Now whisk the egg whites until they form soft peaks, then whisk in the sugar – approximately 1 oz at a time. When all the sugar is in, whisk in the cornflour and vinegar, then spoon the meringue mixture on to the baking sheet, forming a circle about 8 inches in diameter. Place the baking sheet in the oven, turn down the heat to gas mark 1 (275°F) and let the Pavlova cook for 1 hour.

Then turn the heat off, but leave the meringue inside the oven until the oven is quite cold. This operation dries the meringue out beautifully.

Peel the paper away from the base of the meringue, place on a serving dish, and just before serving spread whipped cream over the top and arrange the peach slices all over. Dust with a little icing sugar and serve.

Cardinal Peaches

For four people:

4 large ripe peaches	½ lb raspberries (can be bought
1 tablespoon caster sugar	frozen, but must be thawed)
Vanilla essence (or a pod)	Flaked almonds
2 oz caster sugar	

Wash the peaches and place them whole and unpeeled in a large saucepan. Pour in just enough water to cover them, add 1 tablespoon caster sugar, 2 drops vanilla essence (or a vanilla pod), bring to simmering point, and simmer for 10 minutes. Drain the peaches, slip off their skins and allow them to cool.

Meanwhile sprinkle the raspberries with the caster sugar, leave them for 20 minutes, then press them through a nylon sieve to make a purée.

Place the peaches in a serving bowl (or 4 individual dishes), pour the raspberry purée over, chill thoroughly and serve sprinkled with flaked almonds.

Peaches in Chambéry

To serve four:

4 firm ripe peaches
Juice of a small orange
Juice of ½ lemon

5 tablespoons Chambéry (or
other dry French Vermouth)

Wash the peaches, halve them and remove the stones. Then slice them (leaving the skins on), arrange the slices in a serving dish, then sprinkle in the lemon and orange juice and finally the Vermouth. Cover the dish with foil and chill very thoroughly for several hours. Serve them just as they are.

Pears in Red Wine

To serve six:

6 large pears (as hard as
possible)
¾ pint red burgundy
¼ pint water
4 oz sugar
2 whole cinnamon sticks

1 vanilla pod
1 level dessertspoon
arrowroot
Toasted flaked almonds
¼ pint double cream, whipped

Pre-heat the oven to gas mark ½ (250°F).

Take a good thick casserole large enough to hold the pears. Peel them, but leave the stalks on, and lay them in the casserole. Put the wine, water, cinnamon and sugar into a saucepan and bring it all to the boil. Adding the vanilla pod, pour the lot over the pears. Put the lid on the casserole, then into the oven with it, and let the pears bake very slowly for about 3 hours, turning them over half-way through.

After 3 hours remove the pears and put them into a bowl to cool. Pour the liquid back into the saucepan and remove the cinnamon sticks and the vanilla pod. Mix 1 dessertspoon arrowroot to a smooth paste with a little cold water and add it to the liquid. Gently bring to the boil (stirring all the time with a wooden spoon) and it should thicken slightly and become syrupy. Pour the syrup over the pears and let it all cool, then baste each pear a bit so that they all get a good coating of syrup. Now put them into the refrigerator to get thoroughly chilled, and serve them sprinkled with toasted almonds, and with a bowl of whipped cream on the table.

Plum and Soured Cream Flan

For four to six people:

6 oz sweet shortcrust pastry	3 egg yolks
1 lb dessert plums	½ teaspoon mixed spice
10 oz (2 cartons) soured cream	2 oz demerara sugar
1 oz caster sugar	1 teaspoon ground cinnamon

Pre-heat the oven to gas mark 6 (400°F), with a baking sheet.

Roll out the sweet shortcrust pastry to line a 10-inch fluted flan tin, then halve the plums and remove the stones. Now beat the soured cream with the caster sugar, egg yolks and mixed spice, then pour this mixture into the flan case and arrange the plums over the top (cut side up). Place the flan on the baking sheet, and bake for 20 minutes, then mix the cinnamon with the demerara sugar, sprinkle it all over the top of the flan.

Now bake for a further 20 minutes, turning the heat up to gas mark 8 (450°F) for the final 5 minutes to brown the top nicely. Serve either warm or cold, just as you like.

Raspberry Shortcake

For four to six people:

1 lb fresh raspberries, carefully picked over and washed (or frozen raspberries, thawed)	1 dessertspoon caster sugar
8 oz plain flour	3 oz butter (at room temperature)
5 oz soft brown sugar	1 level teaspoon baking powder

Pre-heat the oven to gas mark 4 (350°F).

Arrange prepared raspberries in a fireproof baking dish and sprinkle them with caster sugar. Sift the flour and baking powder into a mixing bowl, then lightly rub the butter into it until the mixture becomes crumbly.

Now mix in the soft brown sugar and sprinkle this mixture over the raspberries – very lightly, without pressing down. Smooth the surface evenly, then bake in the oven for 25 to 30 minutes.

Serve either hot or cold with fresh whipped cream.

Summer Pudding

To serve six:

1 lb raspberries	5 oz caster sugar
½ lb redcurrants	7 or 8 medium slices white
¼ lb blackcurrants	bread (from a large loaf)

For this recipe you need a 1½-pint pudding basin.

First, prepare the fruit. The blackcurrants and redcurrants can be separated from their stalks in a matter of seconds if you just hold the tip of the stalk firmly between your finger and thumb then simply slide the stalk in between the prongs of a fork, then push the fork downwards pulling off the berries as it goes.

Wash the fruits – keeping an eye on the raspberries as you do so, extracting any that look a bit musty. Place the fruits and the sugar in a wide saucepan over a medium heat and cook them for about 3 to 5 minutes, only until the sugar has melted and the juices begin to run. It is important not to over-cook the fruit and spoil the fresh flavour.

Remove the fruit from the heat, then line the pudding basin with the slices of bread, overlapping them and sealing well by pressing the edges together: fill in any gaps with small pieces of bread, so that none of the juice can get through. Now pour the fruit in – all except for about a cupful, which you will need for later.

Cover the pudding with another slice of bread, then place a small plate or saucer (one that will fit exactly inside the rim of the bowl) on top, and on top of that put 3 lb or 4 lb of weights, then leave in the refrigerator overnight. Just before serving the pudding, turn it out on to a large serving dish, and spoon the reserved juice all over (this will soak any bits of bread that still look white).

Serve cut into slices, and have a bowl of thick cream on the table to go with it.

Tarte de Desmoiselles Tatin

For four people:

1 lb cooking or dessert apples, peeled, cored and thinly-sliced
4 oz soft dark brown sugar
1 teaspoon ground cinnamon

1 tablespoon melted butter
Shortcrust pastry (made with 4 oz flour, and 2½ oz margarine and lard mixed)

You will need an 8-inch round sponge tin with straight sides (no rim).

First, pre-heat the oven to gas mark 4 (350°F), then prepare the tin by brushing it with melted butter and placing a circle of greaseproof paper round the base (brush that with melted butter too). Now cover the base with brown sugar, pressing it down evenly all over, and quite hard. Sprinkle the cinnamon all over, and next arrange the sliced apples, also pressing them down.

Roll out the pastry approximately ¼-inch thick and, placing the tin over it, cut out a suitably sized circle. Place the pastry on top of the apples, press down gently – then cook in the centre of the oven for 40 minutes, until the pastry is golden.

Allow the tart to get quite cold, loosen it round the edges, place a plate on top and turn it all upside down. Remove the tin and greaseproof paper, and serve with or without cream.

Treacle Tart

To serve four to six people:

Shortcrust pastry (made with 4 oz plain flour, 1 oz margarine, 1 oz lard and a pinch of salt)

4 heaped tablespoons fresh wholemeal breadcrumbs
4 tablespoons golden syrup (this will be easier to measure if you warm the tin first)

Pre-heat the oven to gas mark 5 (375°F).

Line a lightly-greased 8-inch flan tin with the pastry and prick the base with a fork. Place it on a baking sheet in the oven for 5 minutes.

Meanwhile, mix the syrup and the breadcrumbs together. (If you like, you can add some lemon juice to the treacle mixture.) When the 5 minutes are up, pour the mixture into the pastry and spread out evenly. Return to the oven and bake for 25 to 30 minutes.

Traditional Trifle

For six people:

1 pint double cream	Raspberry jam
3 egg yolks	4 fl. oz sweet sherry
1 oz caster sugar	1 large tin raspberries, drained
1 level teaspoon cornflour	2 oz flaked almonds
6 trifle sponge cakes	

In a large glass bowl first break the sponge cakes into pieces and spread a little raspberry jam on each piece. Sprinkle in the raspberries and the sherry and stir everything round to soak up the sherry.

To make the custard, heat ½ pint double cream in a small saucepan, then in a basin blend the egg yolks, sugar and cornflour very thoroughly. When the cream is hot, pour it on to the egg mixture, stirring all the time. Now return the custard to the saucepan and stir over a very low heat till it is thick, then remove it – it must not come to the boil or it will curdle.

Pour the custard over the sponge cakes and when it has cooled, spread the other ½ pint cream (whipped) over the top, decorate with flaked almonds and chill for 3 or 4 hours before serving.

10 Cakes, Biscuits and Bread

I am definitely not one of those highly commendable cooks who ritually bake twice a week and produce an endless supply of bread, home-made cakes, buns and biscuits. Sadly, time does not permit. Neither am I at all sure the psychologists are right when they claim that a woman bringing her newly baked cake out of the oven gets all maternal about it and feels she is presenting her husband with a substitute for a new offspring (I'd never be able to raise a knife to it, if I thought that).

However, there are times when I can think of nothing more therapeutic than shutting myself in the kitchen and baking a cake. Even the newly baked aroma that seeps through the house is comforting. I also happen to believe that we have disgracefully neglected one of our proudest meals – British Tea. I hope perhaps some of these recipes may tempt you back into the habit, if only at week-ends.

Apple Crumble Cake

For the cake part:
4 oz self-raising flour, sifted
Salt
2 oz butter (at room temperature)
2 oz caster sugar
1 egg, lightly beaten
2 drops vanilla essence
Milk
2 large cooking apples, peeled and sliced

For the crumble part:
3 oz self-raising flour
2 oz caster sugar
1 oz butter (at room temperature)

1 dessertspoon ground cinnamon
1 dessertspoon soft dark brown sugar

Pre-heat the oven to gas mark 4 (350° F) and grease and line with greaseproof paper an 8 in. round cake tin.

Get two large mixing bowls, and in the first prepare the crumble mixture by rubbing the butter with the flour until it comes fine and crumbly. Add the sugar, then sprinkle in 1 dessertspoon cold water and mix with a fork until the mixture is coarse and lumpy.

Put this aside for a moment and prepare the cake base by creaming the butter and sugar until it is pale, light and fluffy. Now add the beaten egg, gradually, beating all the time; add the vanilla essence as well, then fold in the sifted flour and a pinch of salt. If the mixture looks too dry (it should drop off the spoon with one tap on the side of the bowl), add a drop of milk.

Turn this mixture evenly into the prepared cake tin and arrange the apple slices over it – just lay them lightly on top.

Now put the crumble topping over the apple, place in the centre of the oven and bake for about 1 hour. Leave it to cool for 20 minutes before you remove it from the tin. Finally, mix the cinnamon and brown sugar together and sprinkle over the top.

Banana and Walnut Cake

1½ oz butter
1½ oz lard
4 oz caster sugar
1 egg, beaten
Grated rind of 1 orange and
    1 lemon

8 oz plain flour
2 level teaspoons baking
    powder
4 bananas
2 oz walnuts, roughly chopped

You will need a 9×5-inch loaf tin (well buttered). Pre-heat the oven to gas mark 4 (350°F).

Cream the butter and lard with the sugar till light and fluffy, then beat in the beaten egg a little at a time, and then add the grated rinds. Now, sift the flour and baking powder, and fold it into the creamed mixture. In a separate bowl mash the bananas to a pulp, and add them to the cake mixture, with the chopped walnuts.

Spoon the cake mixture into the prepared tin, level it off on top, and bake for approximately 50 to 55 minutes, or until a skewer inserted in the centre comes out clean.

Squidgy Chocolate Cake

8 oz plain chocolate
5 oz caster sugar
8 large eggs
2 oz cocoa powder

¾ pint double cream
2 tablespoons water (or rum)
½ bar Cadbury's Bournville
    Flake, for decoration

For this you need an oblong baking tin, 11½×7 in., and just over 1 inch deep, lined with greaseproof paper.

For the chocolate filling
Break the chocolate in squares into a basin, and add the water (or rum). Place the basin in a warm oven at gas mark 3 (325°F) and allow the chocolate to melt – about 15 minutes. Then remove it from the heat and beat with a wooden spoon until smooth. Allow to cool, then separate two eggs and beat the yolks first on their own, then into the chocolate mixture.

Now, whisk the egg whites till stiff, and fold them into the chocolate mixture. Cover the bowl and chill in the refrigerator for an hour or so, while you are making the cake itself.

For the cake.

Prepare the cake tin by oiling it lightly, then line it with a suitably sized piece of greaseproof paper, pleating the corners to make it fit – oil the greaseproof paper lightly too. Pre-heat the oven to gas mark 4 (350°F).

Now separate 6 large eggs, putting the whites into a large mixing bowl and the yolks into a pudding basin. Whisk the yolks with either an electric mixer or a hand whisk until they start to thicken, then add the caster sugar and continue to whisk until the mixture feels thick – but be careful not to overdo it, it should not be starting to turn pale. Now mix in the cocoa powder.

Next, whisk the egg whites till they are stiff and stand up in peaks. At that point, take a metal spoon and carefully fold them into the egg-yolk mixture – gently but thoroughly, making sure you get right down to the bottom of the bowl with the spoon.

Pour the complete mixture into the prepared tin, spread it evenly and bake on a highish shelf for 20 to 25 minutes. After that time the cake will appear to have risen and look puffy, rather like a soufflé (it will not look as if it is cooked, but it is). Remove it from the oven but do not be alarmed as it starts to sink, because it is supposed to. When it has cooled, it will look rather crinkly on the surface.

To turn it out, put a suitably sized piece of greaseproof paper on the table, loosen the edges of the cake all round with a knife, then turn the tin upside down on to the greaseproof paper.

Now, cut the cake evenly in half down the centre so that you have two squares. Take the chocolate filling from the refrigerator and whip up the cream until quite stiff. Using a palette knife spread half the chocolate mixture over one half of the cake – it is very fragile, so be gentle, and if it breaks a bit just ease it back together again.

Spread about a quarter of the cream over the chocolate and place the other half of the cake (again very carefully) on top forming a sandwich (a frying pan slice will assist greatly with this very delicate operation). Spread the rest of the chocolate mixture on top.

Wash the palette knife and use it to cover the whole cake (sides as well) with whipped cream. Decorate the top with the crumbled flake, then, using your pan slice again, transfer the whole cake on to a serving dish which should be placed nearby.

Dundee Cake

5 oz butter (at room temperature)
5 oz caster sugar
3 eggs
8 oz plain flour
1 level teaspoon baking powder
6 oz currants
6 oz sultanas

2 level tablespoons ground almonds
Grated rind of 1 small orange and 1 small lemon
2 oz whole blanched almonds
2 oz glacé cherries, rinsed and cut into halves
2 oz mixed candied peel, finely chopped

For this you need a 7 or 8-inch round cake tin (greased and lined with greaseproof paper). Pre-heat the oven to gas mark 3 (325°F).

Put the butter into a mixing bowl. Add the sugar and beat with a wooden spoon until the mixture is light and fluffy (if you have an electric mixer for this, so much the better). Now whisk the eggs and beat them into the creamed butter and sugar, a teaspoonful at a time. If, while the eggs are going in, it starts to curdle, throw in a teaspoon of flour to help it a bit.

When all the eggs are beaten in, take a large tablespoon and fold in the sifted flour and baking powder. When this is done the mixture should be of a soft, dropping consistency (it should leave the spoon with one sharp tap on the side of the bowl). If it seems too dry, add 1 dessertspoon milk.

Next, carefully fold in all the other ingredients: currants, sultanas, cherries, mixed peel, ground almonds and grated orange and lemon rind. Now spoon the mixture into the prepared cake tin, spread it evenly and, with the back of a dessertspoon, make a slight depression in the centre (to stop it rising too much). Then, just as carefully, arrange the whole almonds in circles all over the top, dropping them on very lightly; if you press too hard they will disappear during the cooking.

Place the cake in the centre of the oven and bake for 2 to 2½ hours. Timings for cakes can never be exact, because ovens vary so much; test it in the centre with a skewer – if it comes out quite clean and there are no sizzling noises (you have to get quite close to listen) the cake is cooked. Allow it to cool before taking it out of the tin. The real thing is not moist and dark like some of the factory-made versions – it should be light in colour and have a crumbly texture.

Sticky Gingerbread

¾ lb plain flour, sifted
6 oz butter
1½ teaspoons ground ginger
2 level teaspoons ground cinnamon
⅛ nutmeg, freshly grated
¼ level teaspoon white pepper

1 level teaspoon bicarbonate of soda
4 tablespoons milk
6 oz black treacle
6 oz golden syrup
6 oz soft dark brown sugar
2 eggs, lightly beaten

Pre-heat the oven to gas mark 3 (325°F). Line a buttered 2-pint loaf tin (approx. 9×5 in.) with greaseproof paper and paint the paper with a little melted butter too. To measure treacle, warm it slightly to make it easier to handle, then measure it in a glass measuring jug.

Sift the flour and spices into a large bowl, then mix the bicarbonate of soda with the milk and set on one side. Now place the black treacle, golden syrup, sugar and butter in a saucepan with ¼ pint water, heat and gently stir until thoroughly melted and blended, but do not let it come anywhere near the boil.

Next, add the syrup mixture to the flour and spices, beating vigorously with a wooden spoon; when the mixture is smooth, beat in the eggs a little at a time, followed by the bicarbonate of soda and milk. Pour the mixture into the prepared tin and bake for 1¼ to 1½ hours until well risen, firm to the touch and shrunk away slightly from the sides of the tin.

Remove the cake from the oven and allow to cool in the tin for 5 minutes before turning out. If possible leave it in a cake tin for 24 hours, and serve in thick slices spread with butter.

Honey and Spice Cake

8 oz plain flour
4 oz butter (at room
   temperature)
3 oz caster sugar
1 level teaspoon ground
   cinnamon
1 level teaspoon ground ginger
¼ level teaspoon ground cloves
Finely grated rinds of 1 small
   lemon and 1 small orange
1 large egg, beaten

3 oz clear honey, warmed
   slightly in the oven for a few
   minutes
1 level teaspoon bicarbonate of
   soda
2 oz mixed peel, very finely
   chopped

Lemon Glacé icing (see below)
6 pieces crystallized ginger,
   finely chopped

Pre-heat the oven to gas mark 3 (325° F).

Lightly butter a 7-inch square cake tin. Sift the flour into a
large mixing bowl, then add the sugar, spices and grated orange
and lemon rinds. Now cut the butter into smallish squares and
rub it into the flour until the mixture resembles fine breadcrumbs.

Next, lightly mix in the beaten egg and then gradually add the
warmed honey (the honey, by the way, should be just warm and
not hot).

In a small basin, mix the bicarbonate of soda with 3 tablespoons
cold water. Stir until dissolved, then add it to the cake mixture
and beat fairly vigorously until the mixture is smooth and soft.
Finally stir in the mixed peel, and spread the mixture evenly into
the prepared tin.

Bake the cake for 30 minutes, or until well risen and springy to
touch. Allow to cool a little, then turn the cake out on to a wire
rack to cool, and store the cake in an airtight tin for a few days.

When you want to serve the cake, ice it with a thin Lemon
Glacé icing, made as follows:

4 oz icing sugar
1½ tablespoons lemon juice

2 tablespoons warm water

Sift the icing sugar into a bowl, warm the water and lemon
juice, then mix until you have a thin consistency that will coat
the back of a spoon. Add more water if necessary.

Place the cake on a wire rack (with a large plate underneath),
and pour the icing all over letting it run down and coat the sides.
Sprinkle the top with the preserved ginger for decoration.

Sticky Parkin

½ lb medium oatmeal	2 oz soft dark brown sugar
¼ lb self-raising flour	1 teaspoon ground ginger
½ lb black treacle (or use half black treacle and half golden syrup)	½ teaspoon bicarbonate of soda
	½ teaspoon salt
	3 fl. oz milk
3 oz pure lard	

Pre-heat the oven to gas mark 3 (325°F). Prepare a loaf tin (9×6 in., and 2 in. deep) by lightly greasing it with melted oil or lard, then line the tin with greaseproof paper and lightly oil the paper.

In a small saucepan gently melt the lard and treacle together over a low heat. Then mix the bicarbonate of soda with the milk in a teacup.

Sift the flour, salt and ginger into a bowl, add the oatmeal and brown sugar, mix everything together evenly, then make a well in the centre.

Now pour in the treacle mixture, followed by the milk mixture – then mix very well and very thoroughly. Spoon the mixture into the lined tin, spreading it out evenly.

Bake in the centre of the oven for 1½ to 2 hours, or until the centre is firm to touch. If you are in any doubt as to whether the cake is cooked, insert a fine skewer into the centre, and if it comes out clean and there are no sizzling noises, the cake is done.

Allow the cake to cool a little, then turn out on to a wire rack. When completely cooled, store the cake in an airtight tin for several days before serving – cut in thick slices and spread with butter.

Rice Cake

4 oz butter (at room temperature)	Grated rind of 1 lemon
8 oz caster sugar	3 eggs, separated
	8 oz ground rice

Pre-heat the oven to gas mark 4 (350°F). Brush a 7-inch round cake tin with melted butter. Line the base and sides with grease-proof paper, then paint the paper with a little melted butter.

Cream the butter and sugar together with the lemon rind until light, pale and fluffy. Separate the eggs and place the whites in a clean, grease-free bowl.

Beat the egg yolks first on their own, then into the creamed mixture, a little at a time, beating vigorously after each addition. Next whisk the egg whites until stiff and fold them carefully into the mixture, together with the ground rice. Spoon the mixture evenly into the prepared tin and bake for about 1 hour. To test if the cake is cooked, pierce the centre with a thin skewer which will come out clean when the cake is cooked.

Sachertorte

This is my version of the famous chocolate cake made at the Hotel Sacher in Vienna. The original recipe is a closely guarded secret.

4 oz butter (at room temperature)	4 oz plain flour
4 oz caster sugar	½ level teaspoon baking powder
4 egg yolks, well beaten	5 large egg whites
10 oz bitter dessert chocolate	2 level teaspoons apricot jam, sieved
¼ teaspoon almond essence	4 oz granulated sugar

Pre-heat the oven to gas mark 2 (300°F). You will need a 7½-inch round cake tin lightly, but thoroughly, greased with butter; also a large mixing bowl. Before you start make sure you have everything assembled round you.

First, break up 6 oz chocolate into a basin, place it over a saucepan of hot water with a very low heat under it and leave it to melt slowly (do not try to hurry it).

Then start creaming the butter thoroughly, adding the sugar and beating the mixture (an electric mixer would be useful) until it is very pale and fluffy, and drops off the spoon or whisk with one slight shake.

Now beat in the egg yolks a little (say about 1 dessertspoonful) at a time, and beat well after each addition. When all the egg yolks are thoroughly beaten in, have a look at the chocolate and if it has completely melted (no lumps) beat it gradually into the creamed butter mixture. Then add the almond essence.

Sift the flour and baking powder, put it all back into the sieve and sift a little over the mixture. Fold it in lightly (using a metal spoon), then sift a bit more, fold it in and so on until it is all incorporated. Next whisk the egg whites till stiff but not dry, and carefully fold them into the mixture, using a metal spoon again.

Now, pour the mixture into the prepared cake tin, level off the top, and put it straight into the oven on the middle shelf. Bake it for 1 hour until firm and well risen.

When the cake is cooked, allow it to cool for 10 minutes in the tin, then turn out on to a cooling rack. Carefully turn it over again, so that it is the right side up. Leave it to get quite cold then spread the sieved apricot jam evenly all over the top and sides (this operation is a lot easier if you warm the jam first).

Now you can make the chocolate icing, and to be absolutely sure of success it is best to use a cooking thermometer (see below).

Start by melting the remaining chocolate (in the same way as above), then take a heavy saucepan and dissolve 4 oz granulated sugar in 4 fl. oz water.

Bring it to just below boiling point, then quickly whisk in the melted chocolate, and beat until smooth. Now immediately insert the thermometer by clipping it on to the sides of the saucepan, and continue stirring the mixture until it reaches 240°F.

At that point remove the pan from the heat at once, pour the icing over the whole cake, using a palette knife to cover the sides completely. This icing sets very quickly, so work fast, and if you have any trouble dip the palette knife into boiling water.

Now leave it alone, and avoid touching it until the icing is thoroughly set, or you will spoil the gloss. At Sachers they serve each slice with a dollop of thick whipped cream – but it is still great without.

Note: If you do not have, or cannot get hold of, a cooking thermometer, you could ice the cake with an ordinary glacé icing, which is made as follows:

4 oz bitter chocolate	2 teaspoons glycerine
4 tablespoons water	5 oz (approx.) icing sugar, sifted

Melt the chocolate with the water in a basin over some barely simmering water, beat in the glycerine, then stir in enough sifted

icing sugar to give a good coating consistency. Then proceed as above.

Simnel Cake

Some say there should be 12 bobbles decorating this traditional Easter cake; others say only 11 – representing the Apostles, with or without Judas. You can take your pick, either way you need:

6 oz butter
6 oz caster sugar
3 eggs, beaten
8 oz sultanas
6 oz currants
2 oz glacé cherries, quartered
2 oz cut mixed peel
1½ lb ready-made almond paste

Grated rind of 1 small orange
    and 1 small lemon
8 oz plain flour, sifted
1 level teaspoon baking powder
1½ level teaspoons mixed spice
3 tablespoons milk
Warmed jam

Pre-heat the oven to gas mark 3 (325°F). Line an 8-inch buttered cake tin with greaseproof paper (also buttering the paper).

Cream the butter and sugar in a bowl until fluffy, then gradually beat in the eggs. Stir in the dried fruits, peel and grated rind, then fold in the flour (sifted with the baking powder and mixed spice), alternately with the milk.

Place half of this cake mixture in the prepared tin, level off and cover with a layer of one-third of the almond paste rolled out to the shape of the tin. Spread the remaining cake mixture over the top. Bake in the centre of the oven, on a baking sheet, for 2 hours, then reduce the temperature to gas mark 2 (300°F) and cook for a further hour (or until a skewer inserted into the cake comes out clean).

Leave to cool in the tin for 15 minutes, turn out on to a wire rack and brush the top with a little warmed jam. Roll out the rest of the almond paste to fit the top of the cake, place on top and trim the edges.

With the trimmings make up 11 (or 12) small balls and arrange them around the edge of the cake. Brush with beaten egg and toast under a hot grill until golden-brown.

BISCUITS

Flapjacks

To make about 10 bars:

4 oz soft light brown sugar
6 oz butter or margarine
1 dessertspoon golden syrup

6 oz porridge oats
Almond essence

Pre-heat the oven to gas mark 2 (300°F).

First, butter a 7½-inch square baking tin, approximately 1¼ to 1½ inches deep.

To start, place the sugar, butter or margarine and golden syrup together in a medium-sized saucepan and heat until the butter has melted. Then remove the saucepan from the heat and stir in the porridge oats and a few drops of almond essence. Now, press the mixture out over the base of the prepared tin, and bake in the centre of the oven for 40 to 45 minutes. Allow to cool in the tin for 10 minutes before cutting into oblong bars. Leave until cold before removing the flapjacks from the tin.

Macaroons

For about 3 dozen biscuits:

6 oz ground almonds
1 oz icing sugar
1 teaspoon ground rice
8 oz granulated sugar
3 standard egg whites

Almond essence
Caster sugar
12 blanched almonds, cut into
    strips
Rice paper

Pre-heat the oven to gas mark 2 (300°F).

First, line two large baking sheets with rice paper, then in a bowl mix the ground almonds together with the sifted icing sugar, ground rice and granulated sugar. Now stir in the unbeaten egg whites and a few drops of almond essence and continue stirring until very thoroughly mixed.

Place the mixture in a forcing bag fitted with a ¾-inch nozzle and pipe out rounds of mixture on to the rice paper, allowing room between each for the biscuits to expand during cooking. Sprinkle each one with caster sugar and top it with a piece of blanched almond. Then bake for about 25 to 30 minutes, or until the biscuits are tinged a light golden-brown.

Leave the biscuits to cool, then strip off the rice paper surrounding each biscuit. If you prefer them crisp, store them in an airtight tin as soon as they have cooled. If you prefer them a bit chewy, leave them overnight before storing in an airtight tin.

Shortbread Biscuits

6 oz plain flour
4 oz butter or margarine

2 oz caster sugar, plus a little extra to sprinkle over

Pre-heat the oven to gas mark 2 (300° F).

Make sure the cooking fat is at room temperature before you start. Rub it into the flour, as for pastry, then add the sugar and by this time it should all be quite soft and will knead into a ball (no liquid needed).

Now roll the paste out on a floured board to a thickness of about ⅛ inch. Flour a fluted pastry cutter and cut the biscuits out, then arrange them on a lightly greased baking sheet, and bake for 30 minutes. When they have cooled, dust them with extra caster (or icing) sugar and store in an airtight tin.

BREAD

Wheatmeal Bread

12 oz wheatmeal flour	2 level teaspoons salt
4 oz plain flour	2 level teaspoons dried yeast
$\frac{1}{4}$ oz lard	$\frac{1}{2}$ pint hand-hot water
2 level teaspoons caster sugar	Cracked wheat

All the ingredients must be measured and weighed carefully and exactly. You will also need a large transparent polythene bag (such as pedal-bin liner), a heaped tablespoon of cracked wheat and a little oil.

Start by placing 1 teaspoon caster sugar in a small bowl, then measure $\frac{1}{2}$ pint hand-hot water on to the sugar. Stir until dissolved, then sprinkle in 2 level teaspoons dried yeast. (Dried yeast keeps for about three months stored in an airtight container, but when it gets too old it will not activate.)

Give the mixture a few quick stirs then leave it for about 10 minutes to allow the yeast to dissolve and form a good frothy head. Meanwhile, place the flours in a large mixing bowl with 2 level teaspoons salt and 1 level teaspoon caster sugar.

Mix everything together thoroughly, then lightly rub in $\frac{1}{4}$ oz lard (this small addition of lard helps to keep the bread moist). Now make a well in the centre of the dry ingredients and pour in the yeast mixture when ready, plus the rest of the water you measured – always pour all the liquid in at once.

Start to mix with a large fork, and finish off with your hands, mixing until you have a smooth dough that leaves the bowl clean. If it seems a little too dry add a spot more water. Now transfer the dough on to a very lightly floured flat surface and start to knead it. All you do is stretch the dough, then fold it towards you, pushing it down, then back away from you with the palm of your hand or your fist. Give the dough a quarter turn, then repeat – you can be as rough as you like with it.

Soon the dough will start to feel much firmer and more elastic. Give it about 6 to 10 minutes' kneading altogether, then shape it into two neat rounds (or one large one), place the dough on a lightly greased baking sheet and then brush the surface with some salted water (to help make them crisp when they are cooked). Sprinkle on some cracked wheat if you like.

Next, take a large polythene bag, put a few drops of oil in it and rub it all round the inside of the bag to prevent the dough sticking to it. Now place the baking sheet with the bread dough on it inside the bag, tie it loosely, allowing room for expansion, then leave it in a warm place to rise.

Pre-heat the oven to gas mark 8 (450°F). The baking sheet can be placed near or on top of the stove, which is as good a warm place as any.

In about 30 minutes the dough will have risen to approximately twice its original size; to test it, touch it with your little finger and if it feels very springy, it is ready. Now remove the polythene

bag, place the tray on the middle shelf of the pre-heated oven and bake the bread for about 20 to 30 minutes for small loaves, or 30 to 40 minutes for a large one.

When cooked, the loaf will feel hollow when tapped on the bottom. Transfer it to a wire rack to cool.

Crumpets

To make a dozen:

½ lb strong plain flour
1 level teaspoon salt
1 level tablespoon dried yeast

1 teaspoon caster sugar
½ pint milk
2 fl. oz water

My grandmother used to have some crumpet rings for making crumpets, but alas you can't get them now. However, it is possible to buy egg cooking rings which do very well instead.

First heat the milk and water until it is hand-hot, then dissolve the sugar in it. Mix the dried yeast in with a fork and leave in a warm place for 10 minutes to get a frothy head. Meantime, sift the flour and salt into a mixing bowl, make a well in the centre, then when the yeast is ready pour it all straight in.

Then, take a wooden spoon and gradually mix the flour into the liquid, beating well to make a smooth batter. Now cover the basin with a folded tea towel, and leave it in a warm place for about 45 minutes, by which time the mixture will have become light and frothy.

To cook the crumpets, grease a thick-based frying pan with lard, then thoroughly grease the rings and place them in the pan. Now put the pan over a medium heat and when it is hot spoon 1 tablespoon of the crumpet mixture into each ring, then allow them to cook for 4 or 5 minutes. This is quite an interesting procedure to watch; first you get hundreds of tiny bubbles on the surface, then the bubbles burst and make the traditional holes.

Now, using a spoon and fork, turn the crumpets over and lift off the rings – if they stick a bit, use a tea towel to protect your hands from the heat, and push them through the rings. Then cool the rings and grease them ready for the next four crumpets.

To serve, butter the crumpets generously on the side with the holes. If you have to make them in advance, toast them lightly on both sides before serving.

Spicy Hot Cross Buns

Quantities to make 14 buns:

1 lb plain flour, sifted	3 oz currants
¼ pint milk	2 oz cut mixed peel
1 oz fresh yeast	2 oz caster sugar
1 level teaspoon mixed spice	2 oz butter, melted
1 level teaspoon salt	1 egg, beaten

Pre-heat the oven to gas mark 7 (425°F).

Warm (but do not boil) the milk with ¼ pint water, then in a basin cream the yeast with 2 tablespoons of the warmed liquid. Now stir in the rest and pour over half the flour (sifted into another bowl).

Cover the bowl with polythene and leave in a warm place for 40 minutes – or until the contents have doubled in bulk. Sift the remaining flour with the mixed spice and salt into a separate bowl and add the dried fruits, peel and sugar, followed by the risen yeast mixture. Pour in the melted butter and beaten egg, and mix well.

Now, using your hands, knead the dough until it no longer sticks to the side of the bowl (about 10 minutes) – if it remains sticky add a little plain flour. Cover the bowl again with polythene and leave for 1 hour; then knead vigorously before dividing the dough into 14 round portions and cutting a deep cross into each one with a knife.

Place them on a greased baking sheet (allowing room for expansion) and leave in a warm place for a further 15 minutes, then bake in the oven for 15 minutes. Brush the cooked buns with sugar glaze.

(Note: If using dried yeast, sprinkle 4 level teaspoons yeast into the warm liquid with 2 teaspoons sugar and leave for 10 minutes to allow a good frothy head to form. Then pour the liquid into the flour and continue as above).

Muffins

To make a dozen:

1 lb strong plain flour
1 slightly rounded teaspoon salt
8 fl. oz milk *and*
2 fl. oz water

1 teaspoon caster sugar
2 level teaspoons dried yeast

For this you will need a solid-based frying pan and a little lard.

First, warm the milk and water until it is hand-hot. Dissolve the sugar in it, then sprinkle in the dried yeast. Mix with a fork and leave it for about 10 minutes to get a good frothy head on it.

Now sift the flour and salt into a largish mixing bowl, make a well in the centre, and when the yeast mixture is ready pour it into the well, all at once. Then start to mix it with a fork and finish off with your hands, mixing it to a soft dough that leaves the bowl cleanly.

It is impossible to give exact liquid-to-flour quantities, so if you find the dough a little too sticky sprinkle on a little flour and flour your hands. On the other hand, if it seems too dry, add a spot more water – but *only* a spot.

Now transfer your dough on to a clean surface and then summon all the energy you can to knead it for 10 minutes, until it is very smooth, springy and elastic. Now put the dough back into the bowl, cover with a polythene bag (I find a transparent pedal-bin liner about the right size), and leave it in a warm place until it has doubled in size.

This will take about 30 to 45 minutes, depending on how warm the place is. When it is ready, tip it back on to a clean, lightly floured surface, then take a rolling pin and roll it out to about ½ inch thick. Now, using a 3-inch plain pastry cutter, cut the muffins out – you may need to roll the dough again in between cutting each one out, as it will be very springy and inclined to puff up again.

Mix the scraps and re-roll them to cut out the last muffin, then flour a baking sheet generously – no need to grease it – place the muffins on the sheet, sprinkle them with a little more flour, then leave them to puff up again for about 30 minutes in a warm place.

To cook the muffins, grease a thick-based frying pan with a little lard, heat the pan over a medium heat, then turn the heat down to low and cook the muffins in the pan for about 7 minutes on each side. Unless your pan is extremely large, you will probably have to do this in three separate lots.

All this can be done well in advance, and the traditional way to serve muffins is to break them a little around their waists (but not to open them) and toast them lightly on both sides. The correct way to eat them is to pull, not cut, them apart and insert a lot of butter. They will keep stored in a tin for about 2 days before toasting if you have any left over.

Scones

To make about 12 scones:

8 oz self-raising flour
1½ oz butter or margarine (at room temperature)

¼ pint milk
1½ level tablespoons caster sugar
A pinch of salt

Pre-heat the oven to gas mark 7 (425°F).

With your fingertips quickly rub the fat into the sieved flour. Stir in the sugar and a pinch of salt, then using a knife mix in the milk little by little. When it is all in, flour your hands and knead the mixture into a soft dough – if it feels at all dry, a drop more milk is needed.

Transfer on to a floured pastry board, flour your rolling pin, and lightly roll the dough out to about ¾ inch thick. Take a pastry cutter (1½ or 2-inch, fluted or plain, would be ideal) and tap it sharply to go straight through the dough – do not twist it at all or the scones will go a funny shape.

After cutting as many as you can, knead the dough together again and repeat till it is all used up. If you do not possess a pastry cutter, cut the scones into small triangles with a knife. Place the scones on a greased baking tin, brush the tops with milk and bake them near the top of the oven for 12 to 15 minutes. When they are done, they will have risen and turned golden-brown. Transfer them on to a wire rack, and eat as soon as they are cool. Scones are best eaten fresh, but if you need to keep them, store in an airtight tin and warm them in the oven before eating.

11 Christmas Cooking

Every year as I wash and put away my pudding basins, I vow and declare that I *will* make my Christmas puddings and cakes in August next year, so that they will have time to mature and I won't be panicking in November with all the rest of the Christmas preparations piling up. It is around November, too, that I start to wish it were all over or that we were flying off to the sun for Christmas and I wouldn't have to do a thing.

But really, if that were to happen, I would be miserable because deep-down I love every minute of Christmas cooking and I would hate to miss out on it. It is the one time of the year in our household that we don't want any changes – everything has to be the same, the turkey stuffing, the bread sauce, Christmas pudding, mince pies, trifle and cake, and I'd feel cheated if I could not scoff sausage rolls at two o'clock on Christmas morning after the midnight service.

Traditional Roast Turkey

1 fresh trussed turkey (approx. 12 lb)
4 oz softened butter

6 oz very fat bacon rashers
Salt and freshly milled black pepper

Once the turkey is stuffed (see recipes below), pre-heat the oven to gas mark 3 (325°F), then prepare a very large double sheet of foil, large enough to wrap the turkey in fairly loosely.

Butter the foil, then literally massage the rest of the butter over the skin of the turkey. Be very generous with it, and tuck an extra lump of butter down the sides of the thighs. Season with salt and freshly milled black pepper.

Now arrange the bacon slices over the breast and wrap the foil round securely, but not too tightly (it should encase the bird loosely). Carefully lift the turkey into the roasting tin and place it on a low shelf in the oven. Close the door and let it cook for 3½ to 4 hours.

Towards the end (say after 3¼ hours), remove the foil and the bacon slices, baste the bird quite thoroughly and return it to the oven to brown nicely.

For this last part the heat can be increased to gas mark 5 (375°F). When the turkey is cooked, it can be kept for 10–15 minutes – provided it is in a warm place – while you turn the oven up to gas mark 8 (450°F) to crisp your roast potatoes if you are having them.

(Note: For a smaller or larger turkey, the method is the same; at the same temperature, the timings would be 3¼ to 3½ hours for a bird between 8 and 10 lb, 4½ to 5 hours if it is between 15 and 20 lb.)

Giblet Gravy

The gravy is made with the delicious juices of the bird and some giblet stock. You can make the stock the day before by placing the giblets and the liver in a saucepan, together with an onion cut in half and a scraped carrot, if you have one.

Pour about 1¼ pints water over them, season with freshly milled black pepper and salt, and simmer very gently for 1½ to 2 hours. Then strain into a jug and keep ready for the gravy.

When the turkey is cooked, transfer it on to a large serving dish, keep it warm, then spoon off all the fat from the juices. These should be tipped from the foil into the roasting tin, and when you tilt the tin you will find it quite easy to spoon off the fat (keep it in a bowl – it will come in handy for left-over cooking).

Now sprinkle in 1 level tablespoon flour and stir it into the juices over a low heat. Then add the giblet stock, a little at a time, until you have a smooth fairly thin gravy. Taste to check the seasoning, add a little gravy browning if it needs it, and pour into a warmed gravy boat ready for serving.

Chestnut and Apple Stuffing

Quantities for a 12 lb turkey:

1 large tin natural chestnuts (1 lb 5 oz)
1 lb pork sausage meat
1 lb cooking apples, peeled, cored and chopped small
1 medium onion, chopped small
1 egg, beaten
Salt and freshly milled black pepper

First drain the chestnuts, and in a large bowl mash them with a fork almost to a pulp. Mix them thoroughly with the other ingredients, before adding the beaten egg to bind everything together.

When it comes to actually stuffing the turkey, the best time is the night before. Then keep the bird in a cool place, but not in the refrigerator as it should be at room temperature when it goes into the oven.

Pack the stuffing into the neck end, pushing it up towards the breast – but not too tightly because it expands during the cooking. Gently press in enough to make a nice, plump rounded end, then tuck the neck flap underneath and secure it with a small skewer; the rest can be pushed into the other end.

Pork, Sage and Onion Stuffing

Quantities for a 12 lb turkey:

2 lb pork sausage meat
1 heaped tablespoon chopped
dried sage
1 large onion, chopped small

4 tablespoons white
breadcrumbs
2 to 3 tablespoons boiling
water
Nutmeg, salt and pepper

In a large mixing bowl, mix the breadcrumbs (which are most easily prepared in a liquidizer) with the onion and sage, then add some boiling water and mix thoroughly.

Now work in the sausage meat and, again, mix thoroughly, seasoning with a little salt, some freshly milled black pepper and about a quarter of a nutmeg, freshly grated. If you prefer your stuffing to be crumbly when cooked, leave it as it is; if you like to carve it into slices, then add a beaten egg to bind it all together.

Bread Sauce

To serve five or six people:

3 oz freshly made white
breadcrumbs (after 2 days a
small white loaf with the
crusts cut off will be stale
enough to grate into
breadcrumbs; the best way to
do this is in a liquidizer, if
you have one)

¾ pint milk
1 medium onion
1 bay leaf
15 whole cloves
½ dozen black peppercorns
2 oz butter
2 tablespoons double cream
Salt and pepper

Start the bread sauce off first thing on Christmas morning by cutting the onion in halves and sticking the cloves into the two halves.

Exactly how many cloves you use depends on you, but I like my bread sauce to have a distinctive flavour of cloves (if you really hate the flavour of them, some freshly grated nutmeg would do instead).

Put the onion halves in a saucepan with the milk, a bay leaf and half a dozen whole peppercorns. Now place the saucepan in a warm place for about 2 hours, then over very low heat bring the milk slowly to the boil – this should take about 15 minutes in all. Now remove the onion, bay leaf and peppercorns and reserve them.

Stir the breadcrumbs into the milk, together with 1 oz butter and some salt, and again leave the saucepan on a very low heat, stirring now and then, until the crumbs have swollen and thickened the sauce.

Now put the onion, etc., back into the sauce and leave like that in a warm place until you need it.

Finally, just before serving, remove the onion and spices, beat in the remaining butter and the cream, and taste to check the seasoning.

Roast Stuffed Goose with Prune and Apple Sauce

1 young goose, with giblets

Flour

for the stuffing:
8 oz fresh white
    breadcrumbs
8 oz onions, finely chopped
½ oz fresh sage leaves, finely
    chopped (or 1 level
    tablespoon dried)
2 oz shredded suet
2 eggs, well beaten
Salt and freshly milled
    black pepper

for the sauce:
8 oz prunes, soaked overnight,
    or according to instructions
    on packet
8 oz cooking apples, peeled
    and chopped
½ onion, finely chopped
¼ teaspoon powdered cloves
2 pinches powdered mace
2 level tablespoons caster sugar

Pre-heat the oven to gas mark 7 (426°F.)

First make the stuffing by placing all the ingredients in a mixing bowl, then chop the liver of the goose very finely and add that too. Season very well with salt and freshly milled black pepper, then bind the mixture together with the eggs. Stuff the mixture into the tail-end of the bird, and secure the gap with a small skewer.

Place the goose in a roasting tin, prick all the fleshy parts with a skewer several times, season well with salt and pepper and dust it with flour all over.

Cook it for 30 minutes, then lower the temperature to gas mark 5 (375°F) and continue cooking for a further 3 hours, pouring excess fat out of the roasting tin two or three times during the cooking. During the last 10 minutes turn the heat right up again to gas mark 8 (450°F) to give the skin a final crisping.

While the goose is cooking, make some stock by simmering the giblets, together with an onion, a bay leaf, and seasoning, in $1\frac{1}{2}$ pints water for 1 to $1\frac{1}{2}$ hours. Then prepare the sauce.

Place in a saucepan the prunes and $\frac{1}{4}$ pint of the water they were soaked in and simmer them till they are soft, then press them through a sieve, extracting and discarding the stones.

Soften the onion in a saucepan with 1 tablespoon goose fat, then stir in the chopped apples and simmer until they are a soft fluffy pulp. Now stir in the sieved prunes, caster sugar and spices, taste to see if you need a little more sugar or spice; re-heat it gently, just before serving the goose.

To serve the goose, lift it out on to a warm serving dish, drain off the last bits of fat from the tin, and make some gravy with the juices and the giblet stock. Serve with the apple and prune sauce separate, give each person a little of the stuffing; the nicest accompaniments would be some crisp roast potatoes and spiced braised red cabbage (p. 144).

Christmas Mincemeat

This recipe makes 6 lb – if that is too much, halve the quantities, or make it all and keep half for next year.

12 oz raisins	Grated rind and juice of 2 oranges
8 oz whole mixed peel, finely chopped	Grated rind and juice of 2 lemons
8 oz sultanas	
8 oz currants	2 oz almonds, shelled and cut into slivers
1 lb cooking apples, peeled, cored and finely chopped	4 teaspoons mixed spice
8 oz shredded suet	$\frac{1}{4}$ whole nutmeg, grated
12 oz soft dark brown sugar	6 tablespoons brandy

Mix everything, except the brandy, together in a large bowl. Mix it all very thoroughly, cover with a cloth and leave it for 48 hours. To prevent fermentation, place the mincemeat in a cool oven, gas mark $\frac{1}{4}-\frac{1}{2}$ (250°F) for 3 hours.

Then allow it to get quite cold, stir in the brandy and pack it into clean jars, cover with waxed discs, seal and label.

Mince Pies

With the following ingredients you can make approximately 20 pies:

1 lb mincemeat	A little milk
2 tablespoons brandy or rum	Icing sugar, sifted
Shortcrust pastry (made with 12 oz plain flour and 7 oz mixed margarine and lard)	

You will require 2½-inch patty tins, a fluted 3-inch pastry cutter and a fluted 2½-inch cutter. Pre-heat the oven to gas mark 6 (400°F).

First, mix the mincemeat with the brandy or rum. Mix thoroughly so that the flavour gets evenly distributed. Now roll out the pastry to about ⅛ inch thick, and cut half of it into 3-inch rounds and half into 2½-inch rounds (rolling up the scraps and repeating until you run out of pastry).

Grease the patty tins lightly and line them with the larger rounds, and fill these with the mincemeat (but not too much, only to the level of the edges of the pastry).

Now, dampen the edges of the smaller rounds of pastry with water and press them lightly in position to form lids. Brush them with milk and make a couple of nips in each one with scissors.

Bake highish in the oven for 25 to 30 minutes until a light golden-brown, then cool on a wire tray and sprinkle with sifted icing sugar. Store in a tin, and before serving warm slightly. You can also make a little rum or brandy butter (see p. 167), which goes down very well with mince pies.

Christmas Pudding

The ingredients below are enough for 2 puddings in 2-pint basins or 4 puddings in 1-pint basins:

4 oz self-raising flour
1 heaped teaspoon mixed spice
½ teaspoon grated nutmeg
¼ teaspoon ground cinnamon
8 oz white breadcrumbs, freshly grated from a stale loaf
1 lb soft brown sugar
8 oz shredded suet
1¼ lb currants
½ lb sultanas
8 oz raisins
2 oz mixed peel, finely chopped

2 oz citron peel, finely chopped (try to buy whole candied and citron peel, if possible)
2 oz almonds, blanched, skinned and chopped
Grated rind of 1 orange and 1 lemon
1 apple, peeled, cored and finely chopped
4 standard eggs
5 fl. oz barley wine
5 fl. oz stout
4 tablespoons rum

First of all, put into a bowl the flour, spices, breadcrumbs, sugar and suet, mixing in each ingredient thoroughly before you add the next. Then, gradually mix in all the fruit, peel and chopped nuts. Finally add the orange and lemon peel and the apple.

In another bowl, beat up the eggs fairly well then mix in the rum, barley wine and stout. Empty the whole lot over the dry ingredients – and stir madly. This mixing is vital so when you get weary enlist the aid of the rest of the family.

It is not possible to be absolutely exact about the quantities of liquid – you may find you need a little more stout. The mixture should be of a good dropping consistency, i.e. fall from the spoon when tapped sharply against the side of the bowl.

When the mixing is done, cover the bowl with a cloth and leave it overnight. Next day, grease two pudding basins and pack the mixture in (you can fill them right to the top). Cover with a square of greaseproof paper together with a square pudding-cloth on top. Tie these first with string round the rims of the bowls, then tie the corners of the cloth together on top.

Steam the puddings for 8 hours (one of them can be kept till the next day, if you have only one steamer) but keep an eye on the water to see that it does not boil away. When the puddings are cooked, remove the greaseproof paper and pudding-cloths and replace with a fresh lot. Store them in a cool, dry place and steam them for a further 2 hours on the great day.

Rum Sauce

For four people:

1½ oz butter	¾ pint milk
2 level tablespoons plain flour	2 to 3 tablespoons rum
1½ tablespoons caster sugar	

In one small saucepan, slowly melt the butter and, in another, warm the milk.

Then add the flour to the butter and stir briskly with a wooden spoon until you have a fairly smooth-looking mixture.

Start to add the warm milk a little at a time, stirring until smooth after each addition. When all the milk is in and the mixture is smooth and creamy, stir in the sugar.

Turn the heat very low, cover the sauce and let it cook for 10 minutes, stirring slowly all the time to prevent it sticking. After 10 minutes add the rum, taste to check if it needs a little more sugar (or rum!), and serve.

Old English Port Wine Jelly

3 to 4 oz granulated sugar	Pared zest and juice of 1 lemon
1-inch piece cinnamon stick	½ oz powdered gelatine
3 cloves	½ pint good-quality ruby port
1 blade of mace	

First, place 3 oz sugar in a saucepan with ½ pint water and the cinnamon stick, cloves, blade of mace and lemon zest. Cover and bring to the boil, then remove from the heat and leave to infuse for 15 minutes or so. Meanwhile, place 4 tablespoons cold water in a small basin and stir in the powdered gelatine.

Leave for 5 minutes to absorb the water, then sit the basin in a saucepan of hot water and leave it until the gelatine melts and the liquid becomes completely clear.

Now strain the spices and zest from the syrup and pass the liquid gelatine and lemon juice, too, through the sieve. Then stir the port into the resulting clear liquid, and taste it (the flavour should be strong and rather more sweet than you would normally have it – this sweetness lessens once the mixture is chilled).

Now stir in more sugar if you think it needs it, and stir until dissolved. Pour the liquid into a jelly mould (1¼ pint capacity), or, alternatively, into 8 stemmed glasses, and leave to set. Serve the jelly slightly chilled.

Christmas Cake

The cake should ideally be made well in advance, say in October. The ingredients are:

1 lb currants
6 oz raisins
6 oz sultanas
2 oz mixed peel, finely chopped
2 oz glacé cherries, rinsed and finely chopped
(All the above ingredients should be put into a bowl the night before you make the cake, mixed with 3 tablespoons brandy; cover with a cloth and leave to soak for at least 12 hours)

2 oz almonds, blanched, peeled and chopped
½ lb plain flour
¼ teaspoon salt
½ teaspoon mixed spice
¼ teaspoon grated nutmeg
1 dessertspoon black treacle
½ lb soft brown sugar
½ lb unsalted butter
4 standard eggs
Grated rind of 1 lemon and 1 orange

You will need an 8-inch round cake tin (or a 7-inch square one); greased and lined with greaseproof paper. Pre-heat the oven to gas mark 1 (290° F).

Start by preparing the almonds and putting the treacle in a warm place to melt a bit. Sieve the flour, salt and spices into a bowl. Now cream the butter and sugar in another bowl until it is light and fluffy – this is hard work, but it is the most important part of making a good cake.

When the mixture is creamed to perfection, beat the eggs and add them, a tablespoonful at a time, beating thoroughly before adding the next. (If it looks at all like curdling, add a little of the flour, which helps to stop this.)

When all the beaten egg is in, fold in the flour and spices, without beating any more, just fold it in bit by bit. Stir in the fruit and nuts and the treacle, and finally the orange and lemon rinds.

Spoon the mixture evenly into the prepared cake tin, using the back of a dessertspoon to spread it all evenly. Make a very gentle depression in the centre. (If you do not intend to ice the cake later, arrange a few whole blanched almonds around the top; just put them on lightly, otherwise they will sink and never be seen again.)

Now tie a band of brown paper around the tin (to give the edges extra protection against the heat). Cover the cake with a suitably sized square of double greaseproof paper with a hole in the middle about the size of a 50p piece. Place the cake on the lower shelf of the oven and leave it there (without opening the door) for about 4½ to 4¾ hours. Test it by putting a skewer into the centre; if it comes out clean and there is no sizzling noise, the cake is cooked.

Store your cake in an airtight tin, and at odd intervals make tiny holes in the top and bottom with a fine skewer and pour in some more brandy.

Sausage Rolls

1 lb pork sausage meat	1 teaspoon sage
½ lb puff pastry	1 egg, beaten with 1
1 medium onion, grated	tablespoon milk

Pre-heat the oven to gas mark 7 (425°F).

Mix the sausage meat, onion and sage thoroughly, then on a floured surface roll out the pastry as thinly as possible into an oblong shape. Now divide the sausage meat into three and make three long rolls the same length as the pastry (sprinklings of flour will take care of the stickiness). Place one roll of sausage meat on to one strip of pastry.

Brush the beaten egg all round, then fold the pastry over and seal it as carefully as possible. Lift the whole thing up and turn it, so that when you put it down the sealed part is underneath.

Press lightly, then cut into individual rolls about 2 inches long. Snip three V-shapes in each roll with scissors, and brush with beaten egg. Repeat the whole process with the other strips of pastry and sausage meat.

Place the rolls on a baking sheet and bake high in the oven for 25 to 30 minutes. Store in a tin and warm slightly before serving.

Hot Spiced Cider

1 quart still dry cider
4 oz soft brown sugar
12 whole cloves
4 whole cinnamon sticks
8 allspice berries

Juice of 1 orange
¼ whole nutmeg, grated
4 small Cox's apples
1 oz butter

Pre-heat the oven to gas mark 5 (375°F).

First, using a small sharp knife, make a small slit around the 'waist' of each apple, then rub each one with butter and place them on a baking tray, and bake for 20 to 25 minutes (they should be softened but not floppy; test them with a skewer).

Pour all the other ingredients into a large saucepan and heat the mixture, stirring quite often and adding the apples half-way through. Do not let it come right up to the boil, but serve it very hot.

To keep the cider really hot without boiling it is probably best to place an asbestos mat under the pan, then when you are ready pour it into a large warmed bowl, and ladle it into glass beer tankards with handles (spoons in the glass will prevent cracking).

12 Marmalade

Seville Orange Marmalade

To make 6 lb marmalade:

2 lb Seville oranges	1 large lemon
4 lb preserving sugar	4 pints cold water

Everything must be weighed and measured exactly. The equipment needed comprises:

A medium-sized preserving pan	A packet of gauze (from the chemist)
6 (1-lb) jam or Kilner jars (washed in soapy water, rinsed and dried)	A piece of string
	An orange squeezer
A cooking thermometer	A very sharp knife

First, measure 4 pints of cold water into the preserving pan and add the juice of the lemon. Then, cut all the oranges in half, squeeze out the juice and pour it in with the water, putting all the pips, and bits of skin and pulp clinging to them on to a piece of gauze about 9 in. square.

This should be placed over a large saucer (to collect any juice). Now tie the gauze round the pips loosely, making a little bag, and attach the bag to the handle of the pan on the end of a piece of string (so that the bag is steeped in the water).

At this point, cut the orange halves into quarters – leave all the pith on – and simply cut each quarter into thinnish strips.

This is rather a boring job, but it does not take that long (I did it in 25 minutes exactly). As each orange quarter is shredded, throw it into the water and orange juice.

When the whole lot is in, put the pan on the stove and simmer very, very gently for 2 hours, by which time the liquid will have reduced by half and the bits of orange peel will crush to a pulp when pressed between the thumb and forefinger (cool before

testing). It is most important that the orange peel should be very tender. If it is not, simmer it a bit longer.

Towards the end of the simmering time, empty the 4 lb preserving sugar into a bowl and warm it through in a low oven. When the peel is tender, remove the bag by cutting the string, put it on to a saucer, then place another saucer on top and squeeze hard so that all the excess juice goes into the marmalade.

When the very last drop is squeezed out, add the warmed sugar and allow to dissolve completely. This is very important, because if it does not dissolve properly the marmalade will turn sugary later on.

Be patient and do not be tempted to turn up the heat, just let the sugar dissolve slowly – it takes about 10 minutes altogether. Once all the crystals have disappeared, you can then turn the heat right up high.

Now clip the thermometer on to the side of the pan with the base immersed in the marmalade, and let it come to a fast 'rolling' boil. Take a wooden spoon and stir now and then to prevent it sticking to the bottom.

Let it boil for 10 to 15 minutes until the temperature reaches 220°F, but just before it reaches the required temperature, spoon a little bit on to a saucer. If when it cools, it wrinkles when you push it with your finger, you have a good set. Then as soon as it reaches 220°F, remove the pan and allow it to cool for 10 to 15 minutes.

Put your jars into a warm oven to heat through, then ladle the marmalade into them. Put in a waxed disc and when cold tie down with Cellophane and elastic bands – and label with the date.

Packs of waxed discs and labels for jam jars can be bought at stationers' shops, but if you are using Kilner jars, they each have their own sealing lid.

(Note: If you do not have – and do not feel like getting – a cooking thermometer, during the fast boiling give the marmalade two or three saucer tests as described; and this is made easier if you chill two or three saucers first in the refrigerator.)

Notes

233

Index